iCONLOGiC ™

v050125
Page Count: 202
9781960604347 (Print Book/KDP)
97819606043471 (VitalSource PDF)
9781960604354 (eBook/Kindle)

TechSmith Camtasia:
The Essentials (2025 Edition)

Kevin Siegel

iCONLOGiC™

Contents

NOTES

NOTES

NOTES

iCONLOGiC™

About This Book

This Section Contains Information About:

NOTES

The Author

Kevin Siegel is the founder and president of IconLogic, Inc. He has written hundreds of step-by-step computer training books on applications such as *Adobe Captivate, TechSmith Camtasia, Articulate Storyline, Articulate Rise, iSpring Suite, Adobe RoboHelp, Adobe Presenter, Adobe Technical Communication Suite, Adobe Dreamweaver, QuarkXPress,* and *Adobe InDesign.*

Kevin served for five years in the U.S. Coast Guard as an award-winning photojournalist and has more than three decades of experience as a print publisher, technical writer, instructional designer, and eLearning developer. He is a technical trainer, a veteran classroom instructor, and a frequent speaker at industry trade shows and conventions.

Kevin holds multiple certifications from Adobe and CompTIA and is a Certified Master Trainer and Certified Online Training Professional (COTP) through the International Council for Certified Online Training Professionals (ICCOTP).

You can reach Kevin at **ksiegel@iconlogic.com**.

IconLogic

Founded in 1992, IconLogic is a training, development, and publishing company offering services to clients across the globe.

As a **training** company, IconLogic has directly trained tens of thousands of professionals both on-site and online on dozens of applications. Our training clients include large and small organizations such as Adobe Systems, Inc., Urogen, Agilent, Sanofi Pasteur, Kelsey Seybold, FAA, Office Pro, Adventist Health Systems, AGA, AAA, Wells Fargo, VA.gov, American Express, Lockheed Martin, General Mills, Grange Insurance, Electric Boat, Michigan.gov, Freddie Mac, Fannie Mae, ADP, ADT, Federal Reserve Bank of Richmond, Walmart, Kroger, Duke Energy, USCG, USMC, Canadian Blood, PSA, Department of Homeland Security, and the Department of Defense.

As a **development** company, IconLogic has produced eLearning and technical documentation for Duke Energy, World Bank, Heineken, EverFi, Bank of America, Fresenius Kabi, Wells Fargo, Federal Express, Fannie Mae, American Express, Microsoft, Department of For-Hire Vehicles, DC Child and Family Services, DCORM, Canadian Blood, Cancer.org, MLB, Archrock, NEEF, CHUBB, Canadian Natural Resources, and Hagerty Insurance.

As a **publishing** company, IconLogic has published hundreds of critically acclaimed books and created technical documents for both print and digital publication. Some of our most popular titles over the years include books on Camtasia, HTML, Dreamweaver, QuarkXPress, PageMaker, InDesign, Word, Excel, Access, Publisher, RoboHelp, RoboDemo, iSpring Suite, Presenter, Storyline, Rise, Captivate, and PowerPoint.

You can learn more about IconLogic's varied services at **www.iconlogic.com**.

Book Conventions

At IconLogic, we believe people learn best by doing, not just by watching or listening. With that philosophy in mind, our books are created by instructors and authors with years of experience training adult learners.

IconLogic books feature a minimal amount of text and are packed with hands-on activities, screen captures, and Confidence Checks to help reinforce newly acquired skills.

This book is organized into modules, and because each module builds on lessons taught in the previous one, we recommend completing them in order for the best learning experience.

Lesson Key

Instructions for you to follow look like this:

❑ choose **File > Open**

If you are expected to type anything or if something is important, it is set in bold type like this:

❑ type **9** into the text field

If you are expected to press a key on your keyboard, the instruction looks like this:

❑ press [**shift**]

Confidence Checks

As you work through this book, you will come across the Confidence Check icon at the right. Throughout each module, you are guided through hands-on, step-by-step activities. To help ensure that you are grasping the content, Confidence Checks encourage you to complete a process or steps on your own—without step-by-step guidance. Because some later activities build on what you accomplish during these Confidence Checks, it's important to complete all activities and Confidence Checks in order.

Software & Asset Requirements

To complete the lessons presented in this book, you will need TechSmith Camtasia version 2025 or newer installed on your computer. Camtasia is not included with this book, but you can download a free trial from TechSmith.com.

You will need to download and extract IconLogic's Camtasia projects and media assets that have been created specifically to support this book and this version of Camtasia (see the "Camtasia 2025 Project Assets" section below).

Because you will be importing, recording, and editing audio, ensure that you have a headset or a computer with speakers and a microphone.

You will learn how to incorporate Microsoft PowerPoint presentations into Camtasia projects. To complete those activities, you will need PowerPoint installed on your computer.

NOTES

NOTES

Camtasia 2025 Project Assets

To help you get started with learning Camtasia, I've provided all the project files and media assets you'll need—except for the Camtasia 2025 software itself. I refer to these materials as data files, which include several Camtasia projects, videos, images, audio files, and more. Step-by-step instructions for downloading the data files from my website are provided below.

As you work through this book, imagine that you work for *Super Simplistic Solutions,* a fictional company in Anytown, USA. In your role as the lead corporate trainer and professional eLearning developer, your responsibility is to create all of the corporate training videos using TechSmith Camtasia.

Download and Extract the Data Files

1. Download the support files that accompany this book.

   ❑ start a web browser and go to the following website: **iconlogic.com/data**

   ❑ depending on your platform, click either **PC** or **Mac**

   ❑ from the **TechSmith Camtasia Data Files** area, click the **Camtasia 2025: The Essentials** link

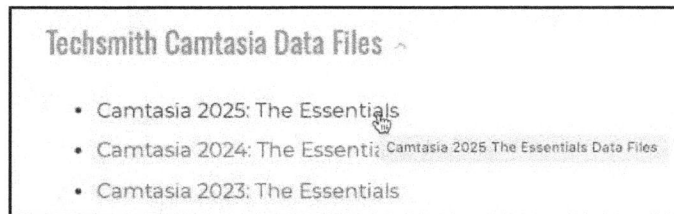

   Techsmith Camtasia Data Files ⌃

   - Camtasia 2025: The Essentials
   - Camtasia 2024: The Essentia   Camtasia 2025 The Essentials Data Files
   - Camtasia 2023: The Essentials

   The download is a zipped file containing several folders and files.

2. Once you have successfully downloaded the assets to your computer, locate and extract the contents of the file. Depending upon which version you downloaded, the file name is either **Camtasia 2025 Book Assets PC or Camtasia 2025 Book Assets Mac.**

   Once unzipped, there should be a folder on your computer named **Camtasia 2025 Book Assets PC** or **Mac.** Shown below is the **Camtasia 2025 Book Assets PC folder.** While the folder structure is identical between the Mac and PC, some of the assets are specific to the Mac or PC operating systems.

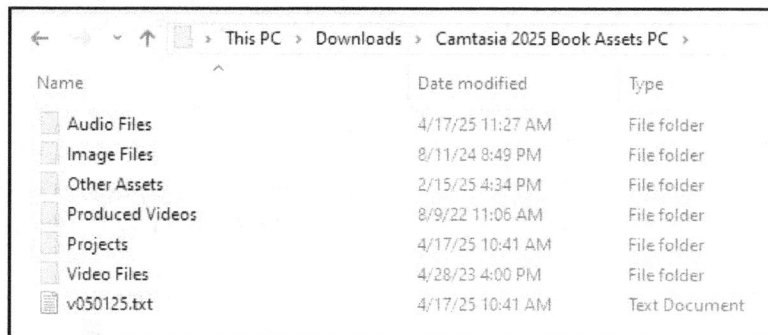

   ← → ⌄ ↑ ▯ ＞ This PC ＞ Downloads ＞ Camtasia 2025 Book Assets PC ＞

Name	Date modified	Type
Audio Files	4/17/25 11:27 AM	File folder
Image Files	8/11/24 8:49 PM	File folder
Other Assets	2/15/25 4:34 PM	File folder
Produced Videos	8/9/22 11:06 AM	File folder
Projects	4/17/25 10:41 AM	File folder
Video Files	4/28/23 4:00 PM	File folder
v050125.txt	4/17/25 10:41 AM	Text Document

How TechSmith Software Updates Affect This Book

This book was written to teach you how to use TechSmith Camtasia 2025 and was published in April 2025. The specific version of Camtasia used for the screenshots throughout this book is 2025.01.

To check which version of Camtasia you're using:

- ❑ On a Windows PC, choose Help > About Camtasia.
- ❑ On a Mac, choose Camtasia 2025 > About Camtasia.

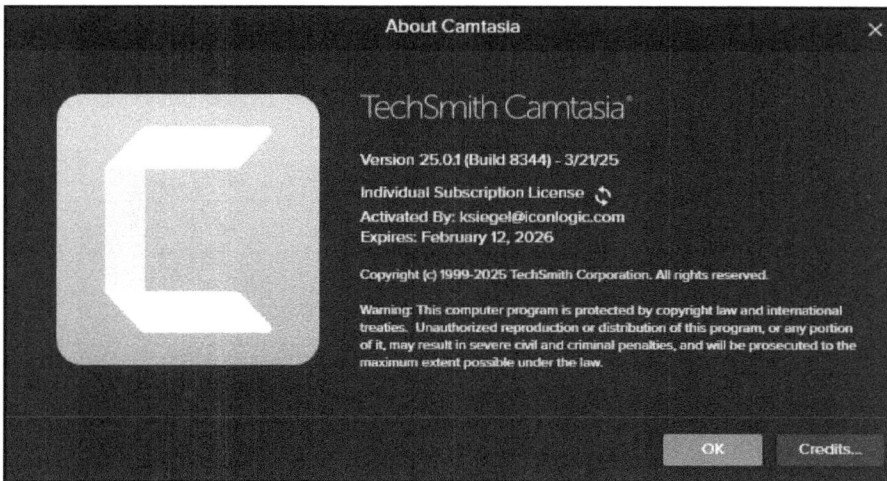

With each significant Camtasia update, I write a corresponding book tailored to that release from TechSmith. Minor updates from TechSmith are typically bug fixes and have little to no impact on the lessons in my books. However, even a minor update can occasionally change how Camtasia looks or behaves. For example, a few years ago, TechSmith released a minor update that introduced new tools and altered several features—these unexpected changes caused confusion for some readers.

Since I can't revise printed books after publication, some instructions in this book may not match your version of Camtasia 2025. If something on your screen differs from what's shown in the book and it's causing confusion, please don't hesitate to contact me at ksiegel@iconlogic.com.

If you're using a newer version of Camtasia than the one I used to create the sample projects, you may see a dialog box asking whether you'd like to update or convert the project files. If that happens, simply follow the onscreen instructions to proceed.

Contacting IconLogic

Web: **www.iconlogic.com** | Phone: **888.812.4827** | Email: **ksiegel@iconlogic.com**

NOTES

Notes

iCONLOGiC™

Rank Your Skills

Before starting this book, complete the skills assessment on the next page.

Skills Assessment

How this assessment works

Below you will find 10 course objectives for *TechSmith Camtasia: The Essentials (2025 Edition)*. **Before starting the book:** Review each objective and rank your skills using the scale next to each objective. A rank of ① means **No Confidence** in the skill. A rank of ⑤ means **Total Confidence**. After you've completed this assessment, go through the entire book. **After finishing the book:** Review each objective and rank your skills now that you've completed the book. Most people see dramatic improvements in the second assessment after completing the lessons in this book.

Before-Class Skills Assessment

1.	I can import media to the Media Bin.	①	②	③	④	⑤
2.	I can add a quiz to a project.	①	②	③	④	⑤
3.	I can create closed captions.	①	②	③	④	⑤
4.	I can export a SCORM-compliant package with Camtasia.	①	②	③	④	⑤
5.	I can record voiceover audio within Camtasia.	①	②	③	④	⑤
6.	I can add hotspots that jump to markers.	①	②	③	④	⑤
7.	I can create a custom animation.	①	②	③	④	⑤
8.	I can use Corner Pin Mode.	①	②	③	④	⑤
9.	I can use the AI Noise Removal tool to improve my audio.	①	②	③	④	⑤
10.	I can record screen actions using the Camtasia Recorder.	①	②	③	④	⑤

After-Class Skills Assessment

1.	I can import media to the Media Bin.	①	②	③	④	⑤
2.	I can add a quiz to a project.	①	②	③	④	⑤
3.	I can create closed captions.	①	②	③	④	⑤
4.	I can export a SCORM-compliant package with Camtasia.	①	②	③	④	⑤
5.	I can record voiceover audio within Camtasia.	①	②	③	④	⑤
6.	I can add hotspots that jump to markers.	①	②	③	④	⑤
7.	I can create a custom animation.	①	②	③	④	⑤
8.	I can use Corner Pin Mode.	①	②	③	④	⑤
9.	I can use the AI Noise Removal tool to improve my audio.	①	②	③	④	⑤
10.	I can record screen actions using the Camtasia Recorder.	①	②	③	④	⑤

IconLogic, Inc.
www.iconlogic.com | ksiegel@iconlogic.com

iCONLOGiC™

Keyboard Shortcuts

Camtasia 2025 is loaded with keyboard shortcuts that make it more efficient to perform common tasks such as adding captions, importing assets to the media bin, and adding animations and effects.

In the pages that follow, I've included screenshots showing all of the available shortcuts. Keep in mind that you can easily customize the default shortcuts.

NOTES

Mac Keyboard Shortcuts

You will find these shortcuts from within Camtasia by choosing **Camtasia 2021 > Preferences** and clicking **Shortcuts**.

Animations and Effects

Add last used transition:	⇧T
Add custom animation:	⇧A
Jump to next animation:	⌥K
Jump to previous animation:	⇧K

Canvas Options

Zoom in on canvas:	⌘=
Zoom out on canvas:	⌘-
Preview media outside of group:	⇧⌘G
Pan to here:	^⌘Z
Scale to Fit:	⌥⌘F
Pan and scale to 200%:	^⌘4
Pan and scale to 100%:	^⌘3
Pan and scale to 50%:	^⌘2
Pan and scale to 25%:	^⌘1

Captions

Add captions:	⇧C

Library Options

Add timeline selection to Library:	⌥⌘A

Marker and Quiz Options

Add marker:	⇧M
Show/Hide marker view:	^M
Next marker:	^]
Previous marker:	^[
Extend selection to next marker:	^⇧]
Extend selection to previous marker:	^⇧[
Add quiz:	⇧Q
Show/Hide quiz view:	^Q
Next quiz:	^0
Previous quiz:	^9

Program Options

Show/hide tools panel:	⌘1
Show/hide properties panel:	⌘2
Open media tab:	B
Open favorites tab:	F
Open library tab:	R
Open annotation tab:	N
Open transition tab:	T
Open behaviors tab:	O
Open animations tab:	A
Open cursor effects tab:	U
Open voice narration tab:	V
Open interactivity tab:	I
Open audio effects tab:	D
Open visual effects tab:	X
Open gesture effects tab:	G
Import package:	^⇧P
Export package:	^⇧E

NOTES

NOTES

Project Options

Import media:	⌘I
Export frame as:	^F
Export Frame at Playhead:	^⇧F
Export:	⌘E

Recorder Options

Start/pause recording:	⇧⌘2
Stop recording:	⌥⌘2

Timeline Editing

Group:	⌘G
Ungroup:	⌘U
Silence audio:	⌥S
Restore audio:	⌥R
Split selected media:	⌘T
Split all:	⇧⌘T
Stitch selected media:	⌥⌘I
Add annotation:	⇧N
Add placeholder:	P
Duration:	^D

Timeline Navigation

Return playhead:	⌃⌥Space
Previous clip:	⌃,
Next clip:	⌃.
Step backward:	,
Step forward:	.
Zoom in:	⇧⌘=
Zoom out:	⇧⌘-
Zoom to fit:	⇧⌘0
Zoom to max:	⇧⌘9
Zoom to selection:	⇧⌘8
Move playhead to beginning:	⌘↩
Move playhead to end:	⇧⌘↩
Extend selection to next clip:	⌥⇧⌘.
Extend selection to previous clip:	⌥⇧⌘,
Extend selection range right:	⇧.
Extend selection range left:	⇧,
Increase track heights:	⌥=
Decrease track heights:	⌥-
Detach/Attach timeline:	⌘3
Open group:	⌃⇧G

NOTES

PC Keyboard Shortcuts

You will find these shortcuts from within Camtasia by choosing **Edit > Preferences** and clicking **Shortcuts**.

Animations and Effects

Add last used transition	Shift+T
Add custom animation	Shift+A
Jump to next animation	Alt+K
Jump to previous animation	Shift+K
Start/stop narration recording	Ctrl+Shift+V

Canvas Options

Zoom in on canvas	Ctrl+=
Zoom out on canvas	Ctrl+-
Enable/disable canvas snapping	Ctrl+;

Program Options

Show/hide tools panel	Ctrl+1
Show/hide properties panel	Ctrl+2
Attach/detach Timeline	Ctrl+3
Open media tab	B
Open library tab	R
Open favorites tab	F
Open annotations tab	N
Open transitions tab	T
Open behaviors tab	O
Open animations tab	A
Open cursor effects tab	U
Open voice narration tab	V
Open audio effects tab	D
Open visual effects tab	L
Open interactivity tab	I
Open captions tab	C
Launch preferences dialog	Ctrl+,
Launch recorder	Ctrl+R
Import Package	Ctrl+Shift+P
Export Package	Ctrl+Shift+E

Project Options

Import into media bin	Ctrl+I
Export frame as	Ctrl+F
Add exported frame to playhead	Ctrl+Shift+F
Produce/share production wizard	Ctrl+P
Silence audio	Shift+S

Timeline Editing

Group	Ctrl+G
Ungroup	Ctrl+U
Open group	Ctrl+Shift+G
Close group	Ctrl+Shift+U
Split selected media	S
Split all tracks at playhead	Ctrl+Shift+S
Stitch selected media	Ctrl+Alt+I
Add annotation	Shift+N
Extend frame	Shift+E
Deselect all	Ctrl+D
Ripple delete	Ctrl+Backspace
Add Placeholder	P
Convert to Placeholder	Ctrl+Alt+P

Library Options

Import to library	Add Shortcut
Add selection to library	Ctrl+Shift+A

NOTES

NOTES

Timeline Navigation

Return playhead	Ctrl+Alt+M
Move playhead to previous clip	Ctrl+Alt+,
Move playhead to next clip	Ctrl+Alt+.
Step backward on timeline	,
Step forward on timeline	.
Zoom in	Ctrl+Shift+=
Zoom out	Ctrl+Shift+-
Zoom to fit	Ctrl+Shift+7
Zoom to max	Ctrl+Shift+9
Zoom to selection	Ctrl+Shift+8
Jump to beginning of timeline	Ctrl+Home
Jump to end of timeline	Ctrl+End
Extend selection to next clip	Ctrl+Alt+Shift+Right
Extend selection to previous clip	Ctrl+Alt+Shift+Left
Extend selection range left	Shift+,
Extend selection range right	Shift+.
Increase track heights	Alt+=
Decrease track heights	Alt+-
Extend selection to timeline beginning	Ctrl+Shift+Home
Extend selection to timeline end	Ctrl+Shift+End
Select succeeding media	Alt+Right
Select preceding media	Alt+Left

Captions

Add caption	Shift+C
Increase caption duration	Ctrl+Alt+]
Decrease caption duration	Ctrl+Alt+[

Marker and Quiz Options

Add marker	Shift+M
Add quiz	Shift+Q
Show/hide marker view	Ctrl+M
Show/hide quiz view	Ctrl+Q
Next marker	Ctrl+]
Previous marker	Ctrl+[
Select next marker	Ctrl+Shift+]
Select previous marker	Ctrl+Shift+[
Next quiz	Ctrl+0
Previous quiz	Ctrl+9

iCONLOGiC™

Preface

In This Module You Will Learn About:

NOTES

Before You Build: Key eLearning Questions

Before launching into Camtasia, take time to plan your eLearning project. Start by identifying the course's purpose and whether eLearning is the right format. Consider your audience—age and experience level can affect how you present content. Not all material works well in eLearning, especially activities like group discussions. If captions are needed, budget extra time for scripting and cleanup. Plan where you'll get visuals, music, and video assets, keeping copyright in mind. If you're using a template, decide whether you'll create it or use a provided one. Also consider who will write any onscreen annotations. Finally, clarify your course type: soft skills training may start in PowerPoint, while software demos need clear, step-by-step scripts.

Why are you creating the course?

You might be surprised by how many people launch Camtasia and immediately start creating content. While well-intentioned, this approach often skips a critical first step: mapping out the entire course, including how you'll track learner comprehension (if that's important to you). During this initial instructional design phase, you might even realize that eLearning isn't the best format for your content and choose a different delivery method.

Who is your audience?

The way children learn is different from the way adults learn. For instance, children often need frequent praise and encouragement during the learning process; however, adult learners might find such praise and encouragement unnecessary—or even irritating. It's also important to determine whether the learner already has foundational knowledge or is new to the topic. The answer to that question can significantly influence the direction of your course content.

Can the lesson work as eLearning?

Not every lesson in an instructor-led course can be effectively repurposed for eLearning. For instance, if a course relies on breakout groups, group discussions, or collaborative work, those aspects are not easily replicated in Camtasia. Remember that eLearners usually work independently and have little or no live interaction with others.

Do you need closed captions?

If your project requires closed captions, you should budget approximately 10–15% more time for their creation in Camtasia—especially if you have a prepared script that can be copied and pasted or if you're using tools like Rev.com to generate SRT files. This estimate is also reasonable if you're using Camtasia's Speech-to-Text feature (PC only), although some manual cleanup will likely be needed. TechSmith Audiate is another powerful tool that can significantly streamline the transcription and captioning process by automatically generating editable text from your audio. However, if you need to transcribe the audio manually without a script, creating captions can take considerably more time—potentially doubling your production effort depending on the length and complexity of the project. Don't forget to account for the time needed to review and fine-tune the captions for timing and accuracy.

Where do you gather assets like music and images?

You will likely need images, videos, and music for your course. But where can you get them? If you search for assets online, be aware that there are likely copyright and usage restrictions. You will learn how to import assets beginning on page 44. You will learn that you can add your own assets and that Camtasia includes a robust number of free assets in the Library. In addition, there are royalty-free assets available via a subscription plan to TechSmith.

Do you need a project template?

You will learn about templates beginning on page 172. If you are required to use a template, are you going to create it, or is it being provided to you?

Will there be onscreen text?

You will learn how to add text to the project (annotations) beginning on page 72. While annotations are easy to insert, who will write the content contained within them? This role is typically filled by a technical writer or technical communicator, professionals skilled at conveying complex information in a clear and concise manner that aligns with the goals of the eLearning course.

What kind of course are you creating?

Are you creating a soft skills course, a software video demonstration, or a marketing video? Soft skills courses typically teach life skills such as conflict resolution, onboarding, or effective interpersonal communication. Video demonstrations, on the other hand, are usually recordings of computer screens. You will learn about recording your screen on page 26.

If your goal is to create soft skills training, does it make sense to build most of the content in Microsoft PowerPoint and then import the presentation into Camtasia? Given PowerPoint's strengths as a presentation tool, I would encourage you to take the PowerPoint route. There are lessons on importing PowerPoint into Camtasia beginning on page 148.

If you're creating a video demonstration, has someone already created a step-by-step script to ensure the correct steps and processes are captured? You'll learn about scripts on page 26.

NOTES

NOTES

Best Practices for Building Engaging and Accessible eLearning

Creating effective eLearning content isn't just about recording a screen or adding a voiceover—it's about delivering a learning experience that's engaging, accessible, and results-driven. Whether you're new to eLearning development or looking to refine your current process, the best projects follow a set of proven practices. These best practices span instructional design, visual layout, accessibility, narration, and even tool-specific tips for platforms like Camtasia. When thoughtfully applied, they help ensure your lessons are clear, consistent, and aligned with how modern learners absorb and retain information. Let's explore the most impactful strategies you can use to elevate your next eLearning project.

Instructional Design Best Practices

☐ Start with learning objectives. Define what learners should be able to do after completing the course. Objectives help shape your structure and assessments.

☐ Keep lessons short and focused. Chunk your content into bite-sized modules (microlearning) to improve learner retention.

☐ Use consistent terminology. Avoid switching terms (e.g., "quiz" vs. "assessment") to minimize confusion.

☐ Respect the limitations of eLearning. Not every instructor-led activity translates well to asynchronous learning. For example, breakout discussions and group collaboration often don't work in standalone video lessons.

Visual and Layout Best Practices

☐ Minimize onscreen clutter. Avoid displaying too much information at once. Keep screens clean and focused on "need-to-know" content.

☐ Avoid overusing bullet points. While they're fine in moderation, consider replacing bullets with a visual per concept—like an image, chart, or diagram.

☐ Split long lists. If you must use bullet points, spread them across multiple screens with supportive visuals.

☐ Use whitespace strategically. Whitespace improves focus and readability.

☐ Stick to a consistent visual style. Apply a uniform set of fonts, colors, and image styles across all lessons.

Accessibility Best Practices

☐ Add closed captions. Ensure audio content is accessible for users with hearing impairments or hardware limitations.

☐ Use high-contrast color schemes. This enhances readability and supports learners with visual challenges.

☐ Avoid fast flashes or excessive animations. These can be distracting—or worse, cause issues for neurodivergent learners.

Audio and Narration Best Practices

- ☐ Use a conversational tone. Talk like you're explaining a concept to a colleague.

- ☐ Record in a quiet space. Poor-quality audio is one of the quickest ways to lose your learner's trust.

- ☐ Keep narration synced with visuals. Ensure what's being said is directly supported by what's on screen.

Camtasia-Specific Tips

- ☐ Use markers to stay organized. Markers help you plan transitions, align content, and manage longer timelines.

- ☐ Name your tracks. Renaming layers in the Timeline is especially useful for more complex projects.

- ☐ Create and use templates. Camtasia templates save time and ensure visual and structural consistency across lessons.

- ☐ Set consistent project dimensions. Choose a project size (e.g., 1280x720 or 1920x1080) and stick with it for uniformity.

- ☐ Choose visuals intentionally. If you're sourcing images online, consider budgeting for paid images to improve quality and save time.

Engagement and Interactivity

- ☐ Add quizzes and checkpoints. This helps reinforce learning and allows learners to assess their progress.

- ☐ Include learner prompts. Encourage learners to take notes or reflect after key lessons.

- ☐ Use effects sparingly. Cursor highlights, zooms, and animations are great—when used purposefully. Avoid overwhelming your audience.

- ☐ Leverage storytelling. Especially for soft skills training, video scenarios or narratively driven examples can boost engagement and retention.

NOTES

NOTES

Fonts and eLearning

The most important thing about eLearning is solid content. But could you be inadvertently making your content harder to read and understand by using the wrong fonts? Is good font selection really important? Read on to discover the many surprising ways fonts can affect your content.

Some Fonts Read Better On-Screen

eCommerce Consultant **Dr. Ralph F. Wilson** did a study to determine if serif fonts (fonts with little lines on the tops and bottoms of characters, such as Times New Roman) or sans serif fonts (those without lines, such as Arial) were more suited to being read on computer monitors. His study concluded that although Times New Roman is easily read in printed materials, the lower resolution of monitors (72 dots per inch (dpi) versus 180 dpi or higher) makes it much more difficult to read in digital format. Times New Roman 12 pt was pitted against Arial 12 pt with respondents finding the sans serif Arial font more readable at a rate of two to one.

Lorem ipsum frangali puttuto rigali fortuitous confulence magficati alorem. Lorem ipsum frangali puttuto rigali fortuitous confulence magficati alorem.	Lorem ipsum frangali puttuto rigali fortuitous confulence magficati alorem. Lorem ipsum frangali puttuto rigali fortuitous confulence magficati alorem.
Times New Roman 12 pt	Arial 12 pt
520	1123
32%	68%

Source: http://www.practicalecommerce.com/articles/100159-html-email-fonts

Wilson also tested the readability of Arial versus Verdana on computer screens and found that in font sizes greater than 10 pt, Arial was more readable, whereas Verdana was more readable in font sizes 10 pt and smaller.

So, should you stop using Times New Roman in your eLearning lessons? Not completely. For instance, you can use Times New Roman for text content that is not expected to be read quickly.

Some Fonts Increase Trust

A study by **Sharath Sasidharan** and **Ganga Dhanesh** for the Association of Information Systems found that typography can affect trust in eCommerce. The study found that to instill trust in online consumers, you should keep it simple: "To the extent possible, particularly for websites that need to engage in financial transactions or collect personal information from their users, the dominant typeface used to present text material should be a serif or sans serif font such as Times New Roman or Arial."

If you feel your eLearning content will be presented to a skeptical audience (or one you've never worked with before), dazzling them with fancy fonts may not be the way to go. You can use fancy fonts occasionally to break up the monotony of a dry lesson, but use such nonstandard fonts sparingly. Consider using the fancy fonts for headings or as accents, but not for the bulk of your text.

The Readability of Fonts Affects Participation

A University of Michigan study on typecase in instructions found that the ease with which a font in instructional material is read can have an impact on the perceived skill level needed to complete a task.

The study found that if directions are presented in a font that is deemed more difficult to read, the task will be viewed as being difficult, taking a long time to complete, and perhaps, not even worth trying. The study also suggests that it is not a good idea to create Camtasia annotations using the Times New Roman font because it could make the content more difficult to process and become overwhelming, especially to beginners.

Popular eLearning Fonts

I ran a poll where I asked developers which fonts they tended to use in eLearning. Here is a list of the most popular fonts:

- ☐ Verdana
- ☐ Arial
- ☐ Calibri
- ☐ Times New Roman
- ☐ Palatino
- ☐ Century Schoolbook
- ☐ Open Sans

NOTES

NOTES

Fonts and Personas

Camtasia's default font is Montserrat, and it can be changed easily using the Properties panel. If you are creating eLearning for business professionals, you might want to use a font that is different from one you would use if you were creating eLearning for high school students. But what font would you use if you want to convey a feeling of happiness? Formality? Cuddliness?

In a study (funded by Microsoft) by **A. Dawn Shaikh**, **Barbara S. Chaparro**, and **Doug Fox**, the perceived personality traits of fonts are categorized. The table below shows the top three fonts for each personality objective.

	Top Three		
Stable	TNR	Arial	Cambria
Flexible	Kristen	Gigi	Rage Italic
Conformist	Courier New	TNR	Arial
Polite	Monotype Corsiva	TNR	Cambria
Mature	TNR	Courier New	Cambria
Formal	TNR	Monotype Corsiva	Georgia
Assertive	**Impact**	**Rockwell Xbold**	Georgia
Practical	Georgia	TNR	Cambria
Creative	Gigi	Kristen	Rage Italic
Happy	Kristen	Gigi	Comic Sans
Exciting	Gigi	Kristen	Rage Italic
Attractive	Monotype Corsiva	Rage Italic	Gigi
Elegant	Monotype Corsiva	Rage Italic	Gigi
Cuddly	Kristen	Gigi	Comic Sans
Feminine	Gigi	Monotype Corsiva	Kristen
Unstable	Gigi	Kristen	Rage Italic
Rigid	**Impact**	Courier New	Agency FB
Rebel	Gigi	Kristen	Rage Italic
Rude	**Impact**	**Rockwell Xbold**	Agency FB
Youthful	Kristen	Gigi	Comic Sans
Casual	Kristen	Comic Sans	Gigi
Passive	Kristen	Gigi	Comic Sans
Impractical	Gigi	Rage Italic	Kristen
Unimaginative	Courier New	Arial	Consolas
Sad	**Impact**	Courier New	Agency FB
Dull	Courier New	Consolas	Verdana
Unattractive	**Impact**	Courier New	**Rockwell Xbold**
Plain	Courier New	**Impact**	**Rockwell Xbold**
Coarse	**Impact**	**Rockwell Xbold**	Courier New
Masculine	**Impact**	**Rockwell Xbold**	Courier New

Source: http://www.usabilitynews.org

eLearning Development Phases

The infographic below offers you a visual guide to the eLearning development process and phases.

A larger version of the graphic can be downloaded from www.iconlogic.com/skills-drills-workbooks/elearning-resources.html. You can also use the camera on your mobile device to scan the code at the right for direct access to the image.

eLearning Development Phases

DISCOVERY

Meet with the client. Find out **what they want** in an ideal eLearning course. Who is the **audience**? Define a course **mission statement** for the course in general. You'll also need a mission statement for each lesson in the course. Will the course require **accessibility**? **Audio**? Will it need to be **localized**? What kind of **hardware** will students be using to access the course?

DESIGN

Which tool will you be using to develop the content (**Camtasia, Captivate, Presenter, Storyline**, or perhaps a combination of a couple tools)? **Instructional design**, a **graphical treatment**, and **navigational choices** are now made and implemented.

WRITING and/or STORYBOARDING

Now that you have chosen a production tool and decided the overall design of the course, you'll need to **plot out the flow** of the course and **write a script and/or a storyboard**. If the course includes voiceover audio, you'll need a separate (and different) script for that.

PRODUCTION

Now it's time to get busy with the **development work** in the selected tool. This includes everything right up to the point of publishing. You'll also **beta test** the lessons in this phase as they are completed.

CLIENT APPROVAL

You're almost there! But, before project completion, you'll need to get your **client's approval**. Depending upon how this goes, **you may need to repeat parts of steps two, three, and four.**

PUBLISHING and IMPLEMENTATION

This includes not only **publishing locally**, but uploading the content to a **web server** or **LMS (SCORM or AICC)**. Be sure to allow time to work out bugs in this phase.

MAINTENANCE

You did a great job! But sometimes changes and updates are necessary. This phase includes **making updates** to the content and **re-posting to the LMS or web server**.

Brought to you by:
ICONLOGIC
www.iconlogic.com

NOTES

NOTES

Camtasia Production Times (Level of Effort)

When I say production time, I'm referring to the actual time you will spend adding content to the Media Bin, adding that content to the Timeline, adding animations, annotations, etc. It may sound like common sense, but the longer the play time for your videos, the longer it will typically take for you to produce them in Camtasia.

Many new eLearning developers underestimate the number of hours needed to produce eLearning. Consider the following guide.

Project Size	Number of Production Hours
Small Videos (1-3 minutes of play time)	1-6 hours
Medium Videos (4-6 minutes)	8-12 hours
Long Videos (7-10 minutes)	14-20 hours
Extra-Long Videos (more than 10 minutes)	Consider splitting videos this large into smaller Camtasia projects.

Project Size and Display Resolution

Several years ago, monitors were small and display resolutions were low—a resolution of 800 x 600 pixels was common. If you developed eLearning content for those smaller displays, a Camtasia canvas size of 640 x 480 worked well.

As display technology improved, 1024 x 768 became the standard resolution, and Camtasia projects typically increased in size to 800 x 600. Today, standard desktop screen resolutions are much higher—often greater than 1366 x 768—and most displays are widescreen (wider than they are tall).

What's the ideal project size for today's learner? Unfortunately, there isn't a one-size-fits-all answer. If you're recording a software demonstration, the width and height of your recording will largely depend on your display size, screen resolution, and the software being recorded. (Some applications cannot be resized and must take up the entire screen.)

Because video card performance and display sizes vary, I prefer to maintain consistency across all my Camtasia courses and recordings. I always use the same computer, screen resolution, Camtasia project template, project size, and screen recording dimensions.

In the image at the right, you can see the Canvas Dimensions available in Camtasia's Project Settings. Based on my experience, project sizes of 1280 x 720 or 1920 x 1080 work best for most learners.

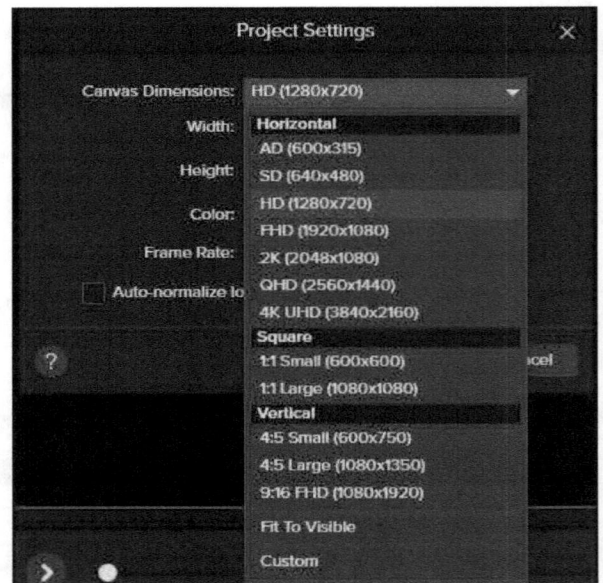

iCONLOGiC™

Module 1: Exploring Camtasia

In This Module You Will Learn About:

- The Camtasia Interface, page 12
- The Media Bin and Library, page 16
- The Canvas and Timeline, page 19
- Reorganizing Tools, page 23

And You Will Learn To:

- Explore a Completed Camtasia Project, page 12
- Explore the Media Bin and Library, page 16
- Use the Canvas to Preview a Project, page 19
- Use the Canvas Edit and Pan Modes, page 22
- Rearrange the Tools, page 23

NOTES

The Camtasia Interface

In these first few guided activities, let's get familiar with the Camtasia 2025 workspace. Specifically, you'll start Camtasia, use the **Home** screen to open an existing project from the Camtasia 2025 Book Assets folder (check the note to the left of this page), and taking a quick tour of the interface.

Guided Activity 1: Explore a Completed Camtasia Project

1. Start Camtasia 2025.

    The **Home screen** opens.

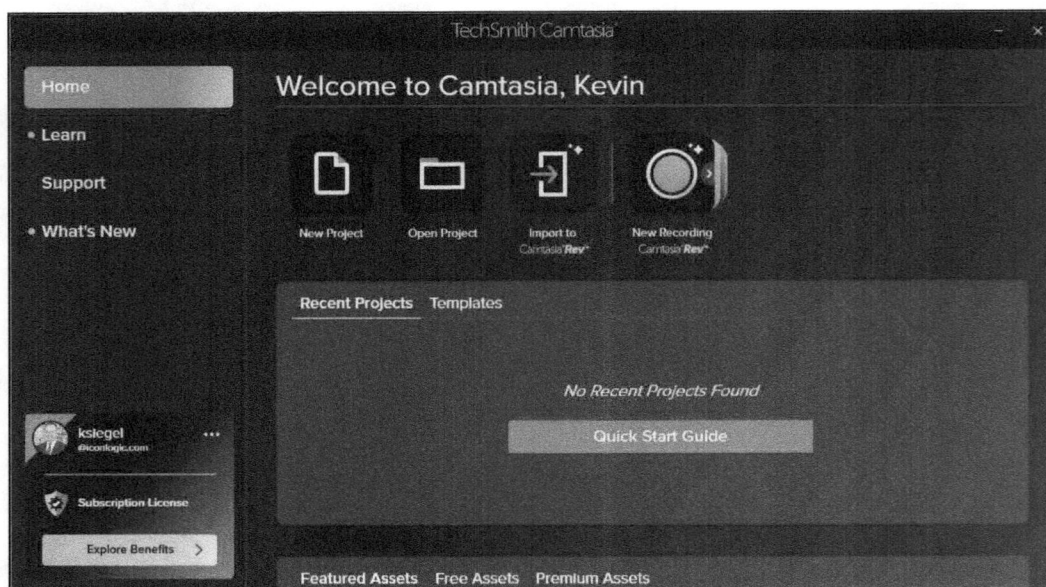

Note: If you have not yet downloaded this book's support assets (Camtasia 2025 Book Assets), turn to the **About This Book** section and work through the **Download and Extract the Data Files** activity on page viii.

2. Open a project from the Camtasia 2025 Book Assets folder.

    ☐ on the **Home** screen, from the options at the left, click **Home**

    ☐ from beneath the heading "Welcome to Camtasia," click the **Open Project** icon

    The **Open** dialog box appears.

    ☐ navigate to the **Camtasia 2025 Book Assets** folder and open the **Projects** folder

    ☐ open the **Demo.tscproj** folder

    ☐ open the **Demo.tscproj** file

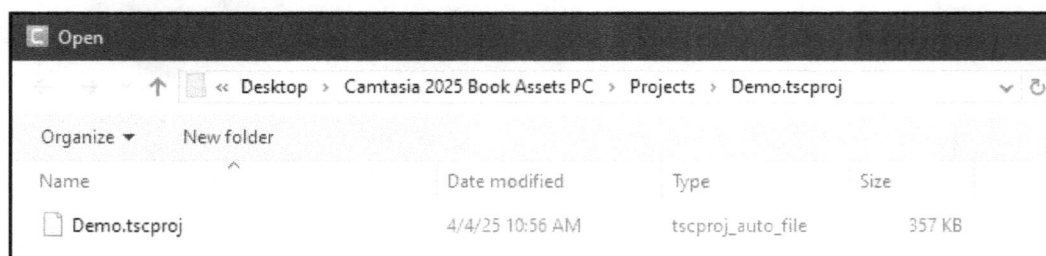

This book was written while using an initial release of Camtasia 2025. Since the book's assets and project files were created, TechSmith has likely released updates to the software. If you see upgrade/convert messages, click **Yes** or **Convert** and acknowledge any upgrade messages as appropriate.

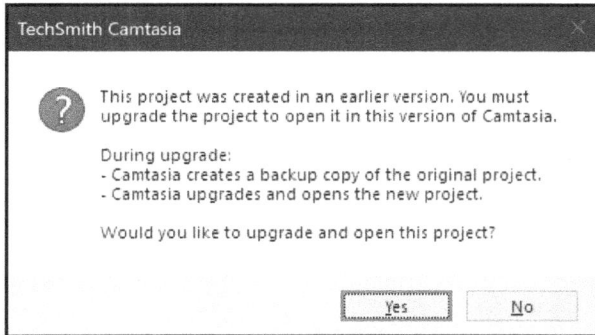

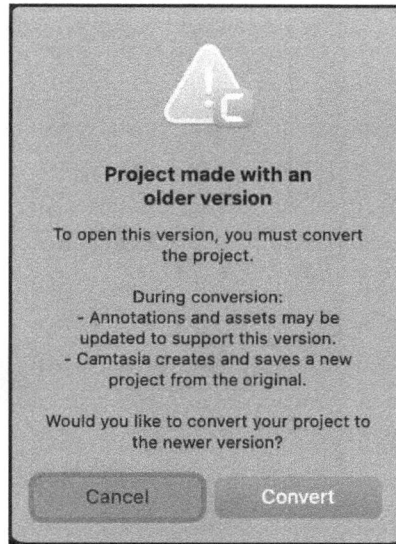

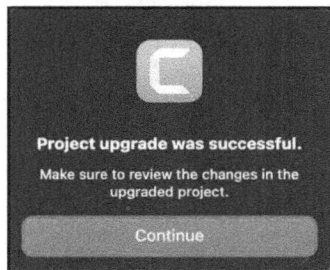

The upgrade/conversion messages are a bit different between the PC and Mac. The images directly above are for the PC. The remaining images are for the Mac. **Mac users:** You will be prompted to Convert the project and immediately specify a save location. Saving to the Camtasia 2025 Book Assets > Projects folder is fine. **PC users:** the save destination is automatically set to the Projects folder.

You will learn to create this project as you work through this book. Let's explore the Camtasia interface and the project components.

NOTES

3. View the voice narration options.

☐ choose **View > Tools > Voice Narration**

The Voice Narration features open. You will learn to record audio beginning on page 100.

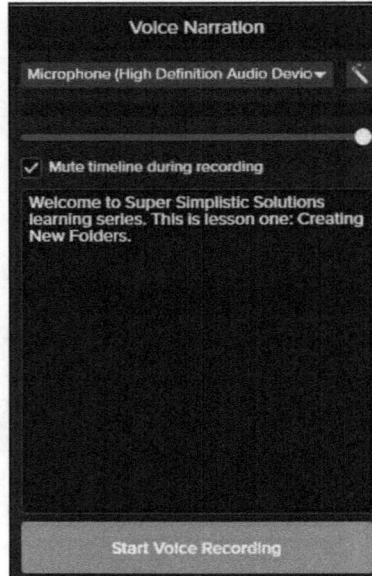

Voice Narration

Microphone (High Definition Audio Devic ▼

☑ Mute timeline during recording

Welcome to Super Simplistic Solutions learning series. This is lesson one: Creating New Folders.

Start Voice Recording

Note: You can access all of the tools from the list of tools at the left. However, depending upon the size and resolution of your screen display, you may need to click **More** at the bottom of the list to see all of the tools.

4. View the annotation options.

☐ from the list of tools at the left, click **Annotations** [🗨 Annotations]

There are six Annotation categories. Annotations are used to focus the learner's attention to specific areas of a video. You will learn to work with Annotations beginning on page 72.

Callouts

Style Basic ▼

Theme None ▼

5. View the transition options.

☐ from the list of tools at the left, click **Transitions** ▭ Transitions

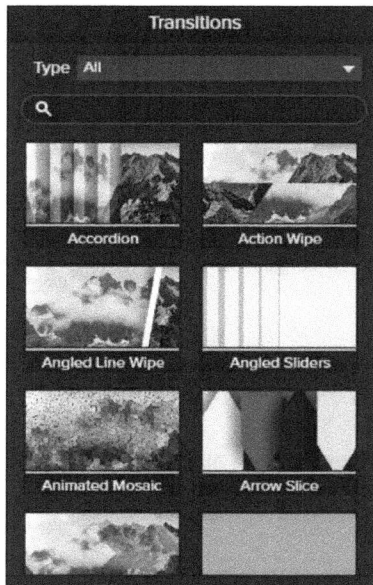

Transitions give you the ability to move from one part of your lesson to another using professional animation effects. You'll learn how to add Transitions to a project beginning on page 85.

NOTES

NOTES

The Media Bin and Library

The Media Bin and Library provide access to media such as images, videos, and audio that can be added to the Camtasia Timeline.

Each Camtasia project has its own Media Bin, which is empty by default. As you import assets into the Media Bin, they can be added directly to the Canvas, the Timeline, or the Library. There is no limit to the number of assets you can add to the Media Bin; however, it cannot be shared with or opened by other Camtasia projects.

The Library comes preloaded with free assets provided by TechSmith, including animations, icons, and music. Unlike the Media Bin, Library assets are available to any Camtasia project on your computer. Additionally, Library assets can be exported and shared with other Camtasia developers on your team.

Guided Activity 2: Explore the Media Bin and Library

1. Ensure that the **Demo** project is open.

2. View the Media Bin.

   ☐ from the list of tools at the left, click **Media**

   ☐ click the **Media** icon

There are several assets in this project's Media Bin, including screen recordings, images, and audio.

The default view for the Media Bin is Thumbnails, which is nice if you want a decent-sized preview of the Media Bin assets. However, many Camtasia users prefer the organized look and feel of the Details view.

3. Change the Media Bin view from Thumbnails to Details.

   ☐ at the bottom right of the **Media Bin,** click the **Change Media Bin view** icon

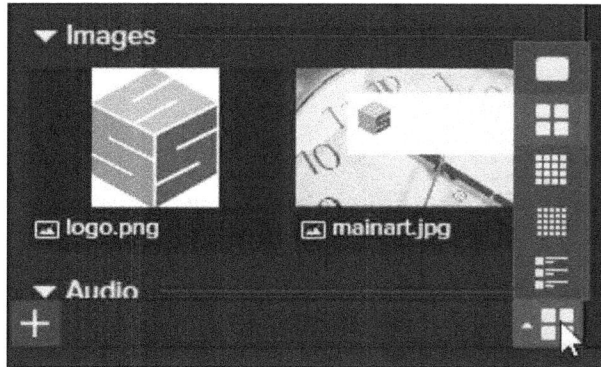

   ☐ click the **Details** icon

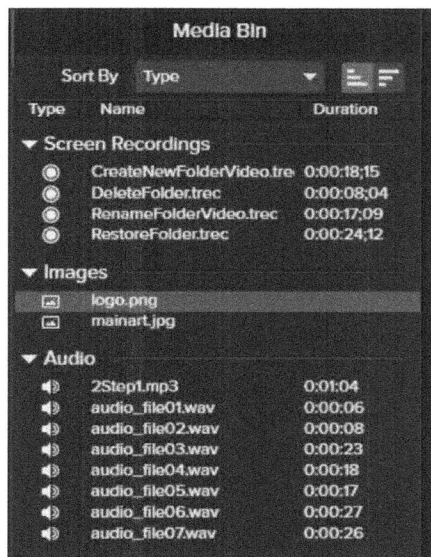

4. Change the Media Bin view from Details back to tiled thumbnails.

   ☐ at the bottom right of the **Media Bin**, click the **Change Media Bin view** icon

   ☐ click the **tiled thumbnails** icon

   You will learn how to add assets to the Media Bin beginning on page 45.

5. View the Library.

   ☐ from above the Media Bin, click the **Library** icon

   The Library takes the space previously occupied by the Media Bin. By default, there are several folders within the Library containing images, animations, and audio files. You can create your own folders and import your own assets into the Library.

NOTES

6. Preview a Library asset.

☐ from the **Library** drop-down menu, choose **Camtasia 2025** (if necessary)

☐ on the **Library**, expand (open) the **Audio** folder

☐ double-click any of the audio assets

A preview window opens, and assuming you have speakers or a headset, you will hear the music.

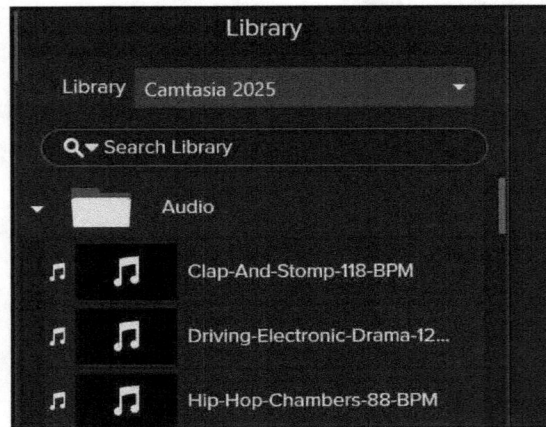

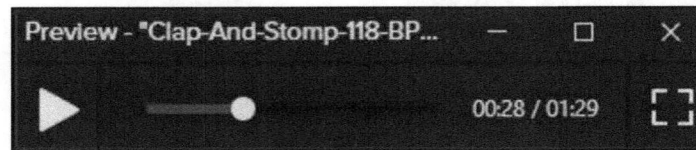

7. Close the audio preview window.

You will learn how to add Library assets to a project later.

The Canvas and Timeline

The Canvas, also known as the stage, offers an excellent way to position screen elements and preview the project as you're working. As you preview a project on the Canvas, you'll be able to use the Timeline to keep track of and control the Canvas media.

The Timeline is at the bottom of the Camtasia window. The Timeline is used to control the timing of objects added to the Canvas. For instance, using the Timeline, you can force objects such as images or videos to appear at the same time, or you can force one object to appear as another goes away.

Guided Activity 3: Use the Canvas to Preview a Project

1. Ensure that the **Demo** project is open.

2. Preview the project.

    ☐ from just below the **Canvas**, click **Play** icon

As the preview plays on the Canvas, notice that an object moves across the Timeline. The object is known as the Playhead. The Playhead includes a thin vertical line and a green and a red square, which you will learn about later. The Playhead and thin vertical line show you where the Canvas preview is at any specific point in time. You will learn to work with the Timeline as you move through the lessons in this book.

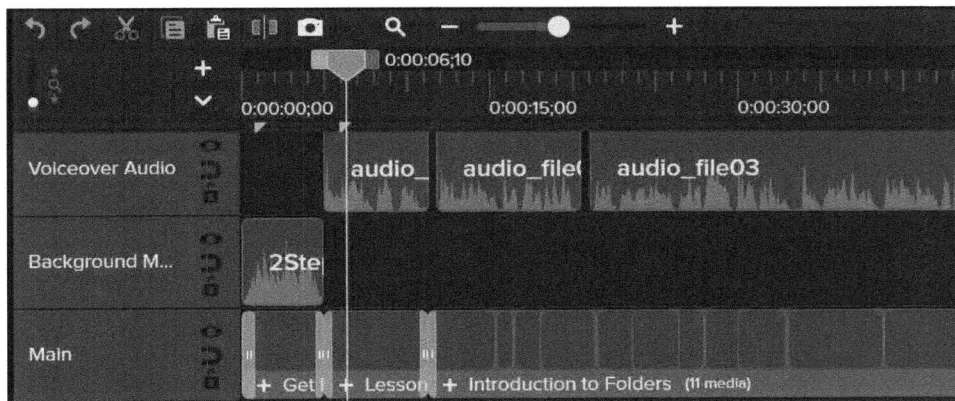

3. Detach the Canvas.

    ☐ choose **View > Canvas > Detach Canvas** (you can click the **Detach Canvas** option in the **Canvas Options** drop-down menu located just above the Canvas)

NOTES

With the canvas detached, you can now position the canvas anywhere on your screen or, if you're using multiple monitors, drag the canvas from one screen to the other.

4. Explore Full Screen Mode.

   ☐ with the Canvas detached, click the **Full Screen** icon (it's in the lower right of the detached Canvas)

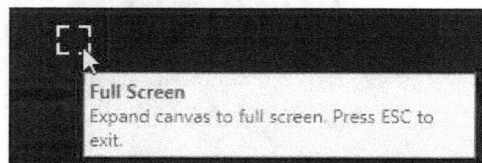

While in Full Screen mode, you can see the lesson but not the Camtasia interface.

5. Exit Full Screen mode.

   ☐ press [**esc**] on your keyboard

6. Attach the Canvas.

   ☐ choose **View > Canvas > Attach Canvas**

The Canvas reattaches itself to the Camtasia window.

7. Use a keyboard shortcut to Zoom closer and farther away from the Canvas.

   ❐ PC users, press **[ctrl] [=]** a few times to zoom closer to the Canvas
   Mac users, press **[command] [=]** a few times to zoom closer to the Canvas

   ❐ PC users, press **[ctrl] [-]** a few times to zoom away from the Canvas
   Mac users, press **[command] [-]** a few times to zoom away from the Canvas

8. Modify the Canvas zooming keyboard shortcuts.

   ❐ PC users, choose **Edit > Preferences**
   Mac users, choose **Camtasia 2025 > Settings**

   The Preferences dialog box opens.

   ❐ select the **Shortcuts** tab

   ❐ select **Canvas Options**

   ❐ to the right of **Zoom in on Canvas**, click the current keyboard shortcut

   ❐ PC users, replace the shortcut with **[ctrl] [shift] [period]**
   Mac users, replace the shortcut with **[command] [shift] [period]**

Zoom in on canvas	Ctrl+Shift+.	↺

Zoom in on canvas:	⇧⌘.	↺

   ❐ PC users, click the **OK** button; Mac users, close the Shortcuts dialog box

9. Test the modified keyboard shortcuts.

   ❐ PC users, press **[ctrl] [shift] [period]** a few times to zoom closer to the Canvas;
   Mac users, press **[command] [shift] [period]** a few times to zoom closer to the Canvas

   ❐ PC users, press **[ctrl] [-]** a few times to zoom away from the Canvas;
   Mac users, press **[command] [-]** to zoom away from the Canvas

10. Restore the keyboard shortcuts to their defaults.

    ❐ PC users, choose **Edit > Preferences**;
    Mac users, choose **Camtasia 2025 > Settings**

    The Preferences dialog box reopens.

    ❐ select the **Shortcuts** tab

    ❐ PC users, click the **Restore defaults** button
    Mac users, from the **Shortcut Set** menu, choose **TechSmith Camtasia Default**

    ❐ PC users, click the **OK** button;
    Mac users, close the Shortcuts dialog box

NOTES

NOTES

Guided Activity 4: Use the Canvas Edit and Pan Modes

1. Ensure that the **Demo** project is open.

2. Move Canvas media.

   ❐ on the **Timeline**, click at **approximately** the **45-second mark**

   The Playhead appears on the Timeline where you clicked.

   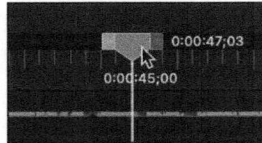

3. Add an arrow to the Canvas.

   ❐ at the far left of the Camtasia window, click **Annotations** [a] Annotations

   ❐ select the arrows tool [↗] and drag any of the arrows onto the Canvas

   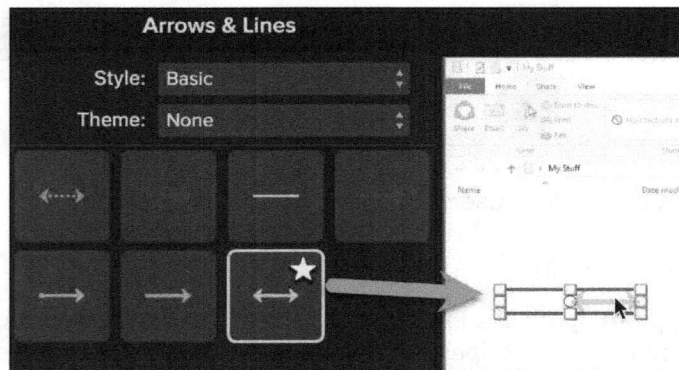

4. Move media around the Canvas.

   ❐ from above the **Canvas**, click the **Edit** mode icon [▶]

   ❐ on the **Canvas**, carefully drag the arrow you just added about an **inch to the right**

   Notice that the media changes Canvas position; the Canvas does not move.

5. Pan the Canvas.

   ❐ from above the **Canvas**, click the **Pan** mode icon [✋]

   ❐ on the Canvas, try to drag the arrow back to the left

   The Canvas pans, but the media does not move.

6. Delete Canvas media.

   ❐ from above the **Canvas**, click the **Edit** mode icon [▶]

   ❐ right-click the arrow you added and choose **Delete** (If the Canvas background disappears, you deleted the wrong media. Choose **Edit > Undo** and try deleting just the arrow again.)

Reorganizing Tools

As you get more comfortable with Camtasia, you will undoubtedly rely on more tools over others. You can easily reorder the tools shown in the list of tools at the left with a quick drag and drop.

> **Note:** The screenshots throughout this book often show the tools in their default order. Feel free to move the tools as you see fit, but keep in mind that some of the screenshots you see as you move through the activities will not match.

Guided Activity 5: Rearrange the Tools

1. Ensure that the **Demo** project is open.

2. Reorganize the tools.

   ☐ from the list of tools at the left, select **Behaviors**

   ☐ drag **Behaviors** and drop it between **Media** and **Annotations**

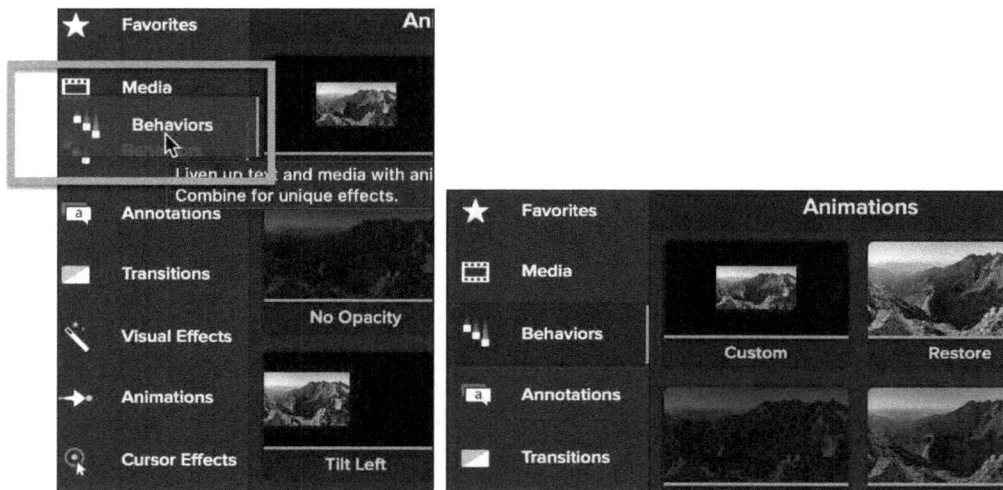

The change to the order of the tools is as immediate as it is permanent. You will see this new tool in this and all Camtasia project. You can easily reorder the tools by dragging and dropping.

3. Exit or Quit Camtasia.

   ☐ PC users choose **File > Exit**;
   Mac users, choose **Camtasia 2025 > Quit**

   If prompted, there is no need to save any changes made to the Demo project.

Notes

iCONLOGiC™

Module 2: Recording Videos

In This Module You Will Learn About:

And You Will Learn To:

NOTES

Rehearsals

During this module, you'll learn how to use Camtasia to record a series of steps you take on your computer. In the next few activities, you'll use either Notepad (PC) or TextEdit (Mac). The process for launching Notepad or TextEdit varies slightly depending on your operating system.

☐ **Windows**: Click **Start** or press the **Windows** key, type **Notepad**, and press [**enter**] to open it.

☐ **Mac**: In Finder, choose **Go > Applications**, then double-click **TextEdit** to open it. If necessary, choose File > New to create a new file.

The Scenario

You have been hired to create an eLearning course that teaches new employees at your company how to use **Notepad** (if you're using Camtasia for Windows) or **TextEdit** (if you're using Camtasia for the Mac). One of the lessons you plan to record using Camtasia includes how to change the page orientation within Notepad or TextEdit.

Step-by-Step Recording Script

Here is a detailed, step-by-step set of instructions you would typically write yourself or receive from a technical/script writer, the Subject Matter Expert (SME), or the instructional designer. As the Camtasia expert, your job will be to perform each step exactly as written below in either Notepad or TextEdit.

1. Start either Notepad or TextEdit. (If necessary, create a new, blank document after starting the program.)

2. From within Notepad or TextEdit, click the **File** menu.

3. Click the **Page Setup** menu item.

4. Click the **Landscape** orientation button.

5. Click the **OK** button.

6. Click the **File** menu.

7. Click the **Page Setup** menu item.

8. Click the **Portrait** orientation button.

9. Click the **OK** button.

The script above sounds simple. However, you will not know what kind of problems you are going to get into unless you rehearse the script prior to recording the process with Camtasia.

Let's run a rehearsal, just as if you were a big-time movie director and you were in charge of a blockbuster movie.

Places everyone, *and quiet on the set.*

Guided Activity 6: Rehearse a Script

1. Start Notepad (PC) or TextEdit (Mac).

Note: In the images on this page, Notepad from Windows 10 is pictured at the left; TextEdit is at the right.

While Notepad from Windows 11 looks a bit different than the classic version of Notepad, the functionality between the Windows 10 and Windows 11 version is the same as it relates to the activities in this module.

2. Rehearse the script.

   ❏ using **Notepad** or **TextEdit** (not Camtasia), click the **File** menu

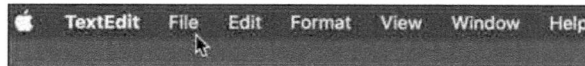

   ❏ click the **Page Setup** menu item

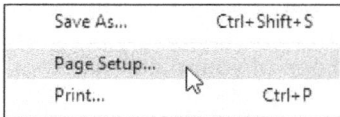

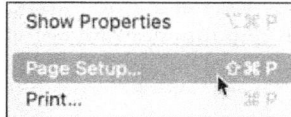

   ❏ from the **Orientation** area, click **Landscape**

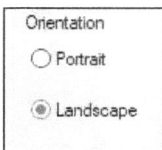

   ❏ click the **OK** button
   ❏ click the **File** menu
   ❏ click the **Page Setup** menu item
   ❏ click the **Portrait** orientation button
   ❏ click the **OK** button

   The script worked perfectly, and there were no surprises. Next, you will work through the same steps again. Only this time, you will record every click with the Camtasia Recorder. As you click, the recorder creates a video of the entire process. That video will be used in the Camtasia editor and serve as the foundation for an eLearning course you will develop during the activities in this book.

NOTES

NOTES

Recording Screen Actions

When recording screen actions using Camtasia, pretend you are using a video recorder or your mobile device to record a movie. You're the director, producer, writer, and actor. Everything you do with your mouse and keyboard is captured during the recording process. Every pause, every good click, bad click, right-click, double-click... everything is recorded. If you move your mouse too inappropriately, your learners will get frustrated by what they see. In the following steps, you will select a recording area on your computer display and then record the process of changing the Page Orientation in Notepad or TextEdit.

> **Note:** While Camtasia is similar on the Mac and PC, recording screen actions differs a bit between the two platforms. I'm showing the two recording processes separately to avoid confusion. PC users, your activities appear below. Mac users, skip ahead to page 34.

Guided Activity 7: Specify a PC Recording Screen and Size

1. Start Camtasia 2025.

2. Start the Camtasia Recorder 2025 tool.

   ☐ with the **Home** category selected on the Camtasia Home screen, click **New Camtasia Video Recording**

   The TechSmith Camtasia Recorder opens. There is a large recording area—the green dashed line—that is likely the size of your primary monitor. There is a horizontal control panel containing **Screen**, **Web Cam**, **Microphone**, **System Audio**, and a red **Rec** button. There is also a Camtasia Rev icon at the bottom right that is likely enabled (green). **Note:** If you have more than one monitor and you do not see the control panel shown in the image below, the control panel could be hiding on one of your other monitors.

3. Select the screen to record.

   ❏ if necessary, click the slider in the **screen** area to allow Camtasia to record the screen

Note: The sliders on the Recorder are toggles. If the slider is positioned left, the option is disabled. If the slider is positioned right (or green), the option is enabled.

   ❏ from the **Screen** drop-down menu, select the screen containing Notepad

The options you see in the menu are dependent upon the number of screens physically connected to your computer. In the image below, I have two screens. My Notepad application is open and positioned on Screen 2.

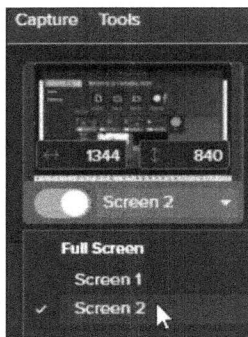

4. Specify the size of the recording area.

   ❏ from the **Screen** drop-down menu, **Horizontal** group, choose **HD (1280x720)**

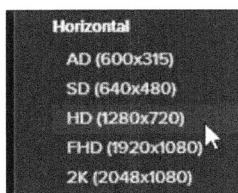

On your screen, the size of the recording area changes to **HD 1280x720 pixels**.

Because modern devices have screens that are typically wider than tall, selecting one of the sizes from the **Horizontal** group makes sense. No law says you must choose one capture size over another. In my experience, HD 1280x720 is currently the more common size used by most fellow eLearning developers. However, the trend is moving toward larger screen captures so **FHD** and **2K** are gaining in popularity. I suggest going with a screen capture size that works well for your needs and be consistent from one recording to the next.

NOTES

NOTES

5. Disable the Camera, Microphone, and System Audio.

   ☐ on the Recorder's Control panel, push the slider for the Webcam, Microphone, and System Audio **left** to disable each of the options

6. Disable Camtasia Rev.

   ☐ on the Recorder's Control panel, click the slider for **Camtasia Rev left** to disable the option

Why disable the camera? If you're considering capturing video of yourself, ask yourself this question: "Is my video enhancing the learner experience?" The honest answer will likely be no.

If the answer is yes, then consider the following and perhaps you'll change your mind.

Are you dressed appropriately? What's behind you? Is there a poster in the background that's inappropriate? If you look good and the background is great, what about the lighting around you? What about your camera angle (is the camera pointed straight up your nose)?

While I don't want you to use your webcam at this point, play around with it later. If you already have videos of yourself on your computer, you can always import them later (you will learn how to import media on page 45).

Why disable the microphone? In my experience, audio and video enhance the learner experience. However, using your microphone now, while you're just learning how to use the Camtasia Recorder, isn't such a great idea. Until you're comfortable recording screen actions, you'll likely end up having to replace the voiceover audio. When teamed with the concentration needed to capture quality screen actions, many people tend to talk too fast, too slow, or flub the voice recording.

You'll learn later that it's easy to import, record, and edit audio from within Camtasia (see page 93). However, once you're comfortable recording video demos with Camtasia, absolutely use your microphone to record your voice while creating the video.

Why disable system audio? I usually disable System Audio because there are few sounds my computer makes that I want included in my Camtasia project. However, if I was recording a virtual meeting—via Zoom or WebEx for example—I would enable System audio so that I captured the audio from the meeting.

Why disable Rev? Rev introduces artificial intelligence (AI) to the video development process. You will get an opportunity to use Rev later.

Guided Activity 8: Create a Software Video Demo on the PC

1. Specify what is to be recorded by Camtasia.

   ❑ on your screen, move and resize the **Notepad** application window as necessary so that the application fits within the 1280x720 Camtasia Recorder capture area

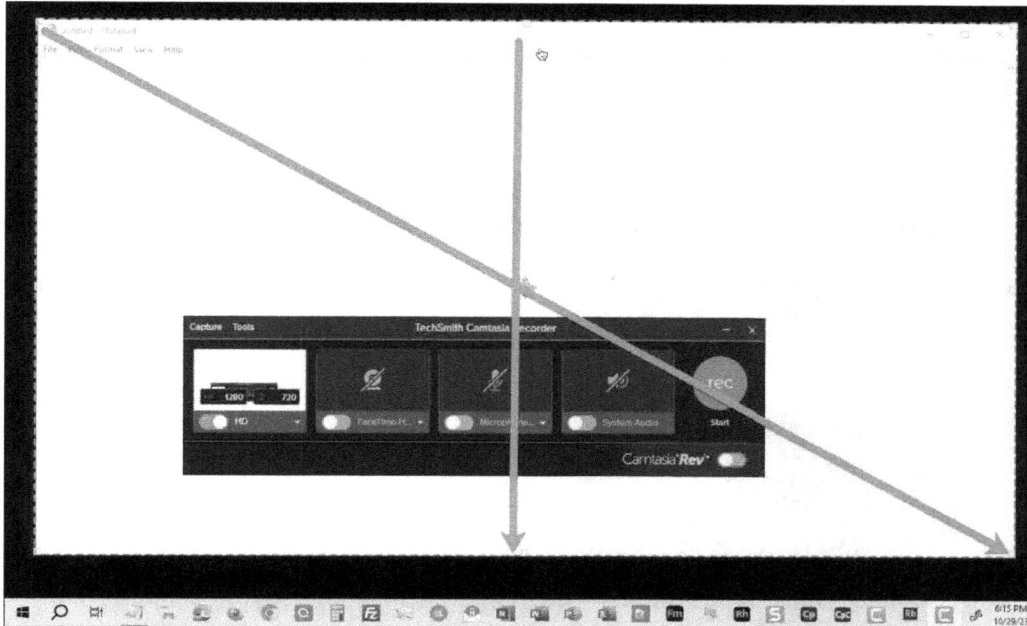

2. Record a software demonstration.

   ❑ on the Camtasia Recorder control panel, click the red **rec** button

   You'll see a three-second countdown.

   ❑ before the counter gets to zero, position your mouse pointer in the **center** of the Notepad window

   After the counter disappears, your every move (and the time it takes you to move) is being recorded.

   ❑ moving steadily (not too fast), move your mouse pointer to the **File** menu
   ❑ click the **Page Setup** menu item
   ❑ from the **Orientation** area, click **Landscape**
   ❑ click the **OK** button
   ❑ click the **File** menu
   ❑ click the **Page Setup** menu item
   ❑ click the **Portrait** orientation button
   ❑ click the **OK** button

NOTES

NOTES

3. Stop the recording process.

☐ on the Camtasia recorder's control panel, click the **Stop** button

Once you stop the recording process, the main Camtasia interface opens. A new Camtasia project is created, and the recording is automatically added to the Camtasia Media Bin. The media is also automatically inserted onto the Timeline.

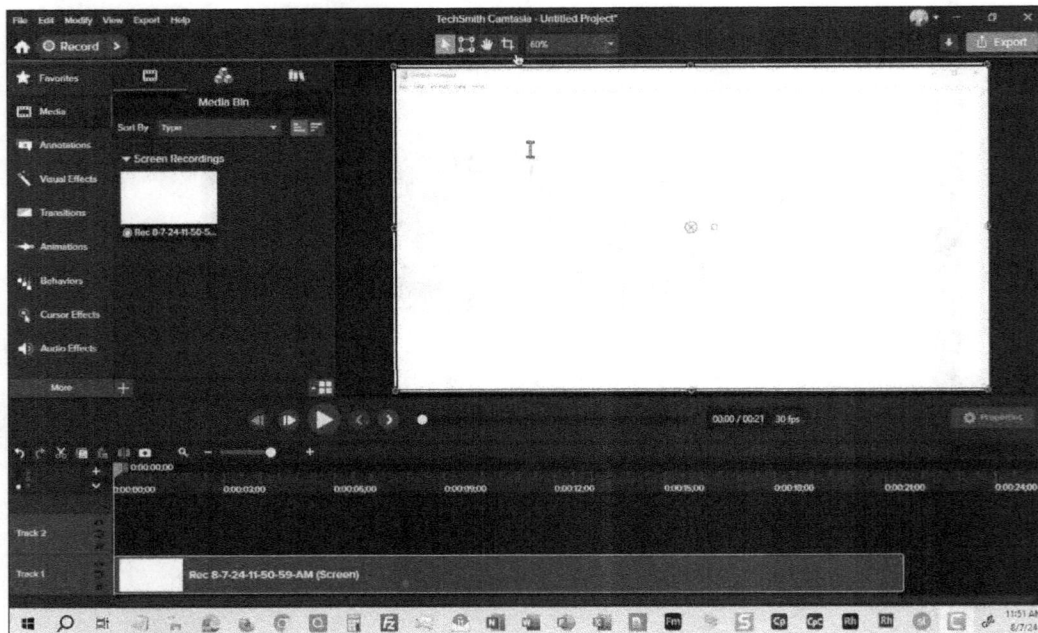

If you'd like to watch the video you recorded, you can use the controls on the Canvas to play and rewind the video as you learned in the last module.

4. View the location of the recording.

☐ on the **Media Bin**, right-click the recording and choose **Open File Location**

The Camtasia folder opens. By default, all of the recordings you create are saved to this folder.

Name	Date modified	Type
Rec 8-7-24-11-50-59-AM.trec	8/7/24 11:50 AM	TREC File

5. Close the window and return to the Camtasia project.

Recording Confidence Check (PC)

1. On the Canvas, preview the project.

   Note: If you are unhappy with the recording, delete the recording media from the **Timeline** (right-click > Delete). Delete the recording media from the **Media Bin** (right-click > Delete). From the upper left of the Camtasia window, click the **Record** icon. Re-record the software demonstration.

2. Save the project to the **Camtasia 2025 Book Assets** folder as **My First Recording.**

   Note: When saving, it's a good idea to ensure that **Create standalone project** is selected. When using this option, all of the media assets used in the project are collected and kept together. Creating a standalone project makes it easier to create a backup of your project on a network or cloud drive and share projects with other Camtasia developers.

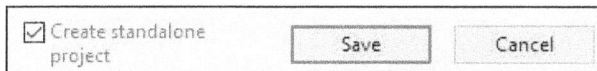

☑ Create standalone project	Save	Cancel

3. Exit Camtasia.

4. Exit the Camtasia Recorder.

5. Exit the Notepad application.

   Note: The rest of this module is for Mac users only. PC users, you can skip ahead to the "Adding Media" module which begins on page 43.

NOTES

NOTES

Guided Activity 9: Set Screen Recording Options on the Mac

1. Start Camtasia 2025.

2. Change Camtasia's Settings so that recordings open in the Editor.

   ☐ choose **Camtasia > Settings**

   | Camtasia | File | Edit | Modify | Text | View | Export |

   About Camtasia
   Manage License...
   Check for Updates...
   ksiegel@iconlogic.com   >
   Settings...   ⌘ ,
   Manage Themes...
   Manage Templates...

   Welco

   The Preferences dialog box opens.

   ☐ from the top of the **Settings** screen, click **Recording**

   ☐ from the **After recording** drop-down menu, choose **Open in Editor** (if necessary)

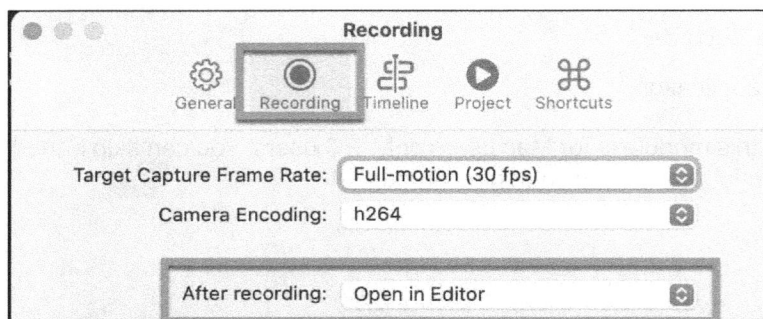

   Recording

   General | Recording | Timeline | Project | Shortcuts

   Target Capture Frame Rate: Full-motion (30 fps)
   Camera Encoding: h264

   After recording: Open in Editor

   With the **Open in Editor** option selected, your recording automatically opens in Camtasia once you stop the recording process.

3. Change the Settings so that recordings are not automatically deleted.

   ☐ if necessary, remove the check mark from **Delete after**

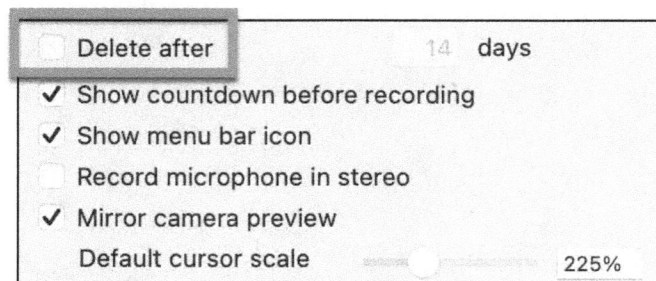

   ☐ Delete after   14   days
   ✓ Show countdown before recording
   ✓ Show menu bar icon
   ☐ Record microphone in stereo
   ✓ Mirror camera preview
   Default cursor scale   225%

   With **Delete after** disabled, recordings won't be automatically deleted from your computer. Assuming you've backed up your projects and project media, consider manually removing older recordings from the Camtasia 2025 folder monthly.

The remaining **Recording** options should match the image below.

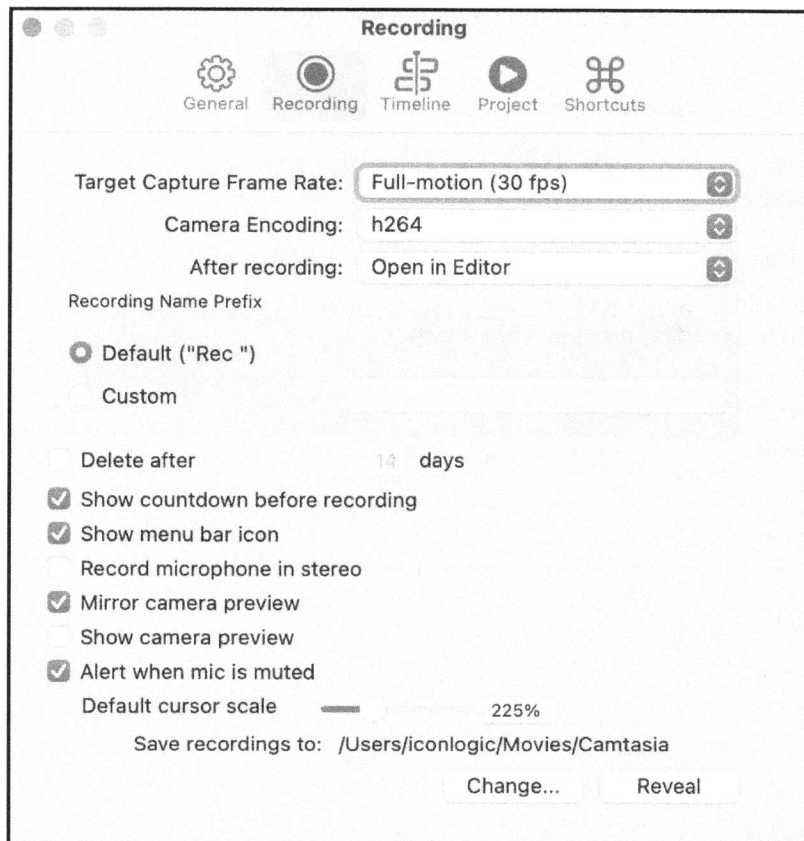

The two most important default Preferences that you did not change are **Target Capture Frame Rate** and **Show countdown before recording**.

By default, recordings are captured at 30 frames-per-second (30 fps). The higher the frame rate, the smoother a recorded video will be. However, when captured at a high frame rate, the file size of a video can be huge, especially if your recording lasts more than a few minutes. If you find that the length of your videos is more than a few minutes, you can experiment with lowering the frame rate prior to recording. This will lower the size of your recording, but could also lower the quality.

Having the **Show countdown before recording** option turned on is a good default. Without this option enabled, the recording process will begin the instant you click the **Start Recording** button—so fast you'll possibly find yourself unprepared and make mistakes while recording.

4. Set a Stop recording Shortcut.

    ❒ from the top of the dialog box, click **Shortcuts**

    ❒ from the list at the left, click **Recorder Options**

    ❒ from the **Shortcut Set** drop-down menu, choose **TechSmith Camtasia Default**.

NOTES

You can stop the recording process by clicking a stop button on the Recorder or use your keyboard. There are two recording shortcuts: **Start/pause** and **Stop**. You can click the shortcut buttons and decide control the keyboard keys that will Start/pause or Stop the recording.

❑ at the right of **Stop recording**, click the button

The Stop recording button enters edit mode. At this point, you could change the shortcut by pressing a key combination on your keyboard.

❑ click away from the Stop recording button to cancel edit mode

❑ make a note of the Stop recording keyboard combination (you will need to use those keys to stop a recording process very soon)

Start/pause recording:	⇧⌘2
Stop recording:	⌥⌘2
New Recording:	^R
Add Marker During Recording:	^⌥⇧⌘M

5. Close the Settings dialog box.

Guided Activity 10: Specify a Mac Recording Screen and Size

1. Ensure that the **TextEdit** application is running.

2. Create a new Camtasia recording.

   ❏ with the **Home** category selected on the Camtasia Home screen, click **New Camtasia Video Recording**

   The Camtasia Recorder opens. There is a large recording area with a green border that is likely the size of your screen. There is a horizontal control panel containing **Screen**, **Web Cam**, **Microphone**, **System Audio**, and a red **Rec** button. There is also a Camtasia Rev icon at the bottom right that is likely enabled (green).

3. Choose a screen to record.

   ❏ if necessary, click the **slider** in the **screen** area to allow Camtasia to record the screen

   Note: The sliders on the Recorder are toggles. Each option is either on or off. Green means the option is enabled; gray means the option is disabled.

   ❏ from the **Screen** drop-down menu, select the screen containing **TextEdit**

   The options you see in the menu are dependent upon the number of screens physically connected to your computer. In the image below, I have two screens. **TextEdit** is positioned on my Built-in Retina Display.

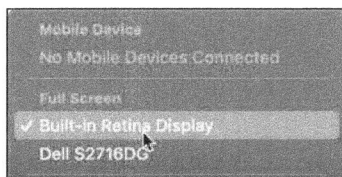

4. Specify the size of the recording area.

   ❏ from the **Screen** drop-down menu, **Horizontal** group, choose **FHD 1080p (1920x1080)**

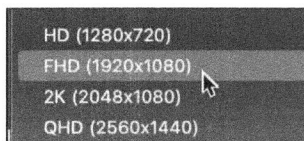

   On your screen, the size of the recording area changes to **1920 x 1080** pixels.

   Most devices have screens that are wider than they are tall. For that reason, selecting one of the sizes from the Horizontal group makes sense. Between the available sizes, the perfect size is debatable. In my experience, 1280x720 is currently the more common size

NOTES

used by eLearning developers. However, the trend is moving toward larger screen captures, so sizes such as 1080p is gaining in popularity. And because 1280x720 is likely too small of a capture size on a Mac's Retina Display, you're going with 1920x1080.

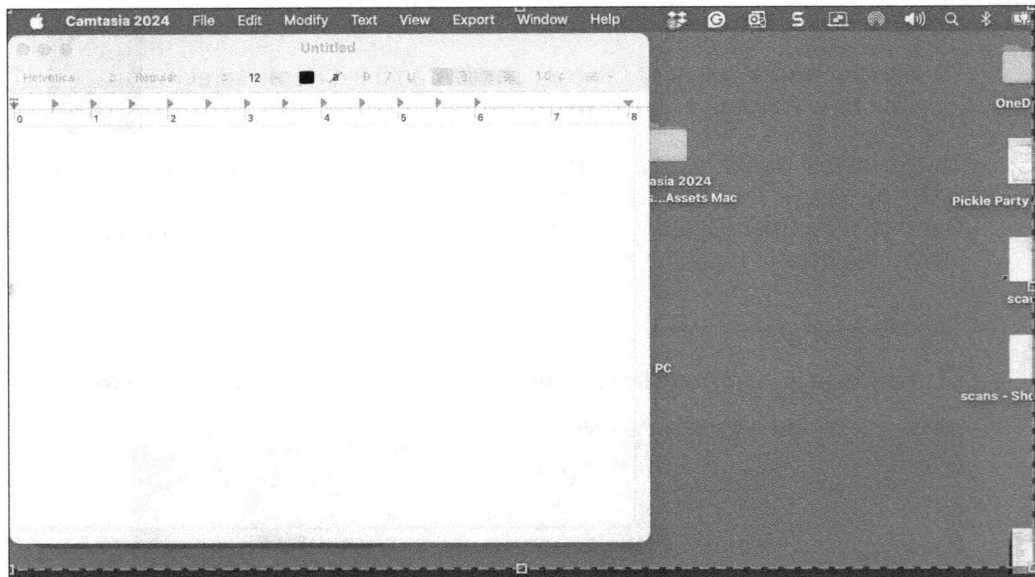

❐ click the **OK** button

5. Select an area of the screen to be recorded.

❐ resize the TextEdit application window as necessary so that both the TextEdit **menu bar** and the TextEdit **application window** fit within the green Camtasia Recording Area

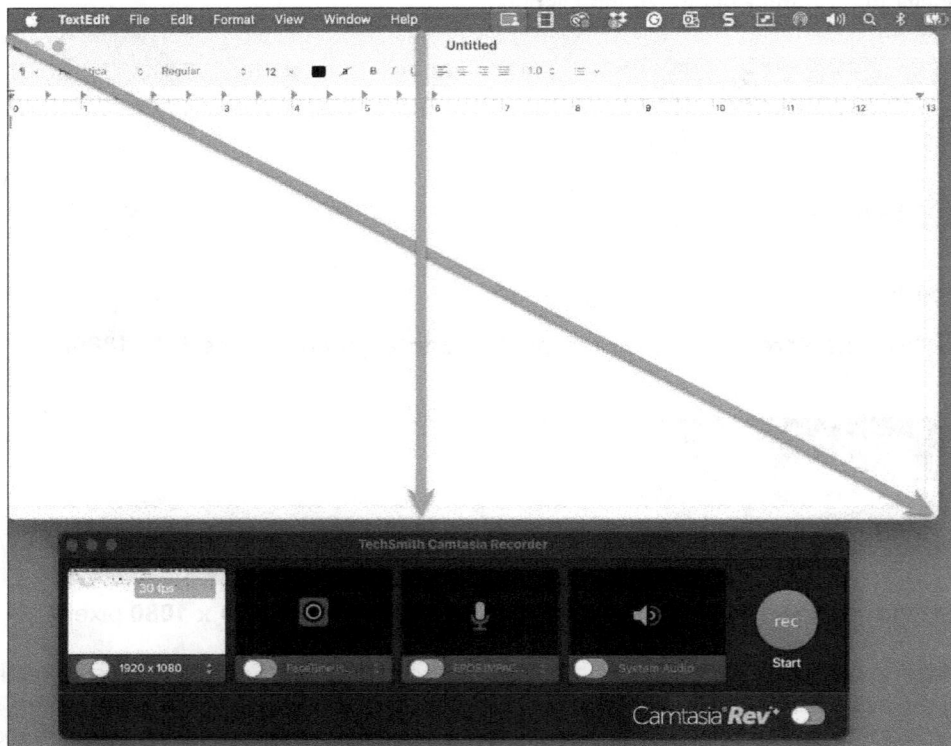

6. Disable the Camera, Microphone, and System Audio.

☐ on the Recorder's Control panel, push the slider for the Webcam, Microphone, and System Audio **left** to disable each of the options

7. Disable Camtasia Rev.

☐ on the Recorder's Control panel, push the slider for Camtasia Rev **left** to disable the option (if necessary)

Why disable the camera? If you're considering capturing video of yourself, ask yourself this question: "Is my video enhancing the learner experience?" The honest answer will likely be no.

If the answer is yes, then consider the following and perhaps you'll change your mind.

Are you dressed appropriately? What's behind you? Is there a poster in the background that's inappropriate? If you look good and the background is great, what about the lighting around you? What about your camera angle (is the camera pointed straight up your nose)?

While I don't want you to use your webcam at this point, play around with it later. If you already have videos of yourself on your computer, you can always import them later (you will learn how to import media on page 45).

Why disable the microphone? In my experience, audio and video enhance the learner experience. However, using your microphone now, while you're just learning how to use the Camtasia Recorder, isn't such a great idea. Until you're comfortable recording screen actions, you'll likely end up having to replace the voiceover audio. When teamed with the concentration needed to capture quality screen actions, many people tend to talk too fast, too slow, or flub the voice recording.

You'll learn later that it's easy to import, record, and edit audio from within Camtasia (see page 93). However, once you're comfortable recording video demos with Camtasia, absolutely use your microphone to record your voice while creating the video.

Why disable system audio? I usually disable System Audio because there are few sounds my computer makes that I want included in my Camtasia project. However, if I was recording a virtual meeting—via Zoom or WebEx for example—I would enable System audio so that I captured the audio from the meeting.

Why disable Rev? Rev introduces artificial intelligence (AI) to the video development process. You will get an opportunity to use Rev later.

NOTES

| NOTES |

Guided Activity 11: Create a Software Video Demo on the Mac

1. Record a software demonstration.

   ☐ on the Camtasia Recorder control panel, click the red **Rec** button

   You'll see a three-second countdown.

   ☐ before the counter gets to zero, position your mouse pointer in the center of the **TextEdit** window and click

   After the counter disappears, your every move (and the time it takes you to move) is being recorded.

   ☐ moving steadily (not too fast, not too slow), move your mouse pointer to the **File** menu
   ☐ click the **Page Setup** menu item
   ☐ from the **Orientation** area, click **Landscape**
   ☐ click the **OK** button
   ☐ click the **File** menu
   ☐ click the **Page Setup** menu item
   ☐ click the **Portrait** orientation button
   ☐ click the **OK** button

Note: If your stop recording keyboard shortcut does not work, you can force the recording to stop by right-clicking the Camtasia icon on the Dock and choosing Stop Recording.

2. Stop the recording process.

   ☐ on your keyboard, press the keyboard combination you set up back on page 36

   Once you stop the recording process, a few things happen in rapid succession. First, the Camtasia Recorder application closes. Second, the Camtasia Editor opens. Third, a new project is created. The recording you created is added to the Camtasia Media Bin and inserted onto the Timeline.

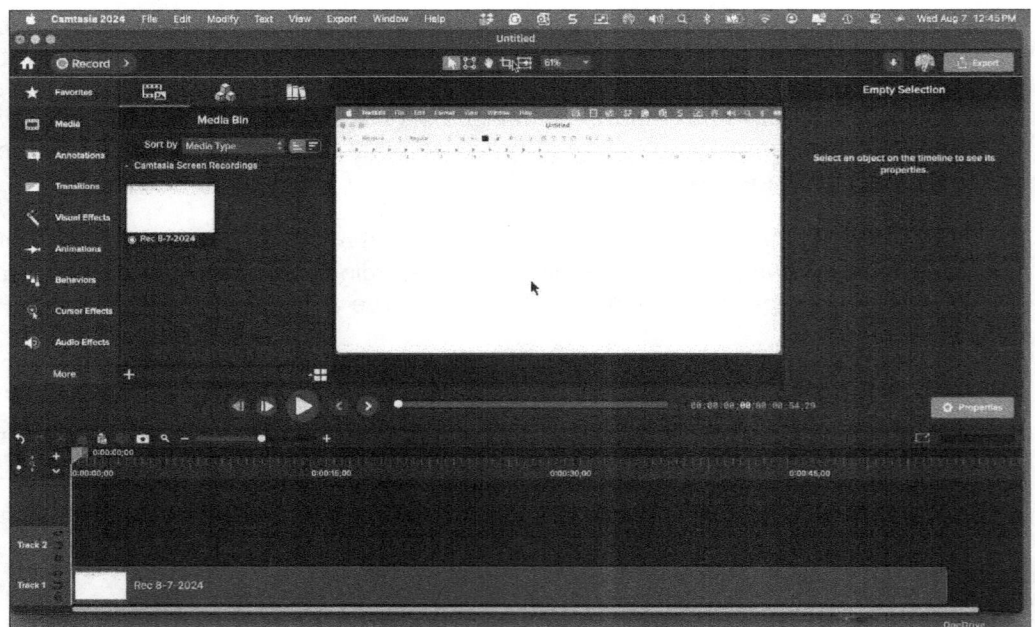

Recording Confidence Check (Mac)

1. On the Canvas, preview the project.

   If you are unhappy with the recording, delete the recording media from the **Timeline** (right-click > Delete). Delete the recording media from the **Media Bin** (right-click > Delete). From the upper left of the Camtasia window, click the **Record** icon. Re-record the software demonstration.

2. Save the project to the **Camtasia 2025 Book Assets** folder as **My First Recording.**

   Note: When saving, it's a good idea to ensure that **Create standalone project** is selected. When using this option, all of the media assets used in the project are collected and kept together. Creating a standalone project makes it easier to create a backup of your project on a network or cloud drive and share projects with other Camtasia developers.

3. On the **Media Bin**, right-click the recording and choose **Reveal in Finder**.

   The Recordings folder opens. By default, all of the recordings you create are saved to this folder.

4. Close the window and return to the Camtasia project.

5. Quit Camtasia.

6. Quit the TextEdit application (there is no need to save the TextEdit document if prompted).

NOTES

Notes

iCONLOGiC™

Module 3: Adding Media

In This Module You Will Learn About:

And You Will Learn To:

NOTES

New Projects and Adding Videos

During the first module of this book, you were introduced to the tools that make up Camtasia and explored the Camtasia interface (beginning on page 12). Then you used the Camtasia Recorder to record screen actions (beginning on page 28). Now you'll create a Camtasia project from scratch, set the canvas dimensions, and add media.

Guided Activity 12: Create a Project and Edit Project Settings

1. If necessary, start Camtasia and ensure that you can see the Home screen.

2. Create a new project.

   ☐ from the **Home** tab of the Home screen, click **New Project**

   Welcome to Camtasia, Kevin

   New Project | Open Project | Import to Camtasia *Rev* | New Recording Camtasia *Rev*

   In a moment, you will add media to the project's canvas. Before adding media, let's visit the Project Settings screen and review the Canvas Dimensions. If you resize the canvas after adding media, you will likely need to go back and resize the media assets on the Canvas.

3. Change the size of the canvas.

   ☐ PC users, choose **File > Project Settings**;
   Mac users, choose **Edit > Project Settings**

   ☐ from the **Canvas Dimensions** drop-down menu, choose **HD (1280x720)**

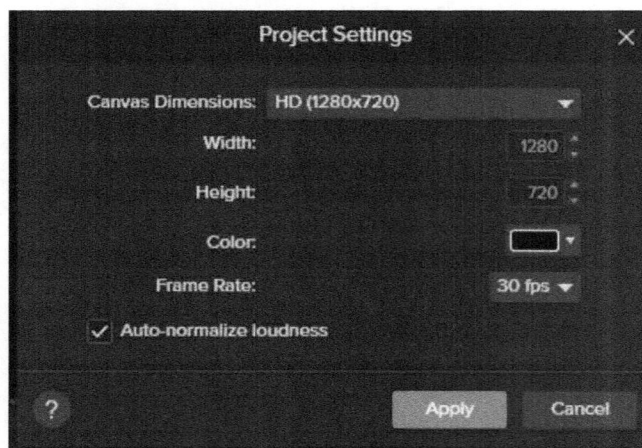

   Project Settings ✕

   Canvas Dimensions: HD (1280x720) ▼
   Width: 1280
   Height: 720
   Color: ▼
   Frame Rate: 30 fps ▼
   ✓ Auto-normalize loudness
   ? Apply Cancel

   ☐ click the **Apply** button

   As mentioned in the last module, most learner displays are wider than they are all tall. A rectangular project size of **1280x720** is very popular. Another popular rectangular project size is FHD **1920x1080**.

Guided Activity 13: Import a Video into the Media Bin

1. Import a video into the Media Bin.

   ❏ from the list of tools at the left of the **Camtasia** window, click **Media** 🎞️

   There are three Media tabs: Media Bin, 🎞️ Camtasia Assets, 🎭, and Library. 📚

   ❏ click the **Media Bin** icon 🎞️ to display the **Media Bin** (if necessary)

   Note: The Media Bin icon on the Mac looks a little different than the PC icon shown above. The Mac version has an additional icon. 🎞️

   ❏ on the **Media Bin**, click the **Import Media** button

   The Open dialog box appears. Any supported video file you can access from your computer can be imported into a Camtasia project using this dialog box.

   Note: If you have not yet downloaded this book's support assets (also known as Data Files), turn to the **About This Book** section at the beginning of this book and work through the **Download and Extract the Data Files** activity on page viii.

   ❏ from the **Camtasia 2025 Book Assets** folder, open the **Video Files** folder

   ❏ open/import **CreateNewFolderVideo**

   You may see an alert message about Proxy Media.

   ❏ click the **OK** button

   When you add videos to a Camtasia project, your computer may slow down while editing due to the high resolution of the video files. To improve performance, Camtasia may automatically create and use a lower-resolution version of the video, known as a proxy. While the video might appear blurry during editing, the final exported content will retain full quality.

NOTES

NOTES

That said, many developers choose to remove the proxy and work with the original high-resolution video instead. If you see a yellow dot on the media thumbnail, it means the video has been added to the project as a proxy. In the images below, the Media Bin on the left shows the proxy icon in the Windows version of Camtasia, while the Media Bin on the right shows the same video without the proxy icon (the Mac version is shown below).

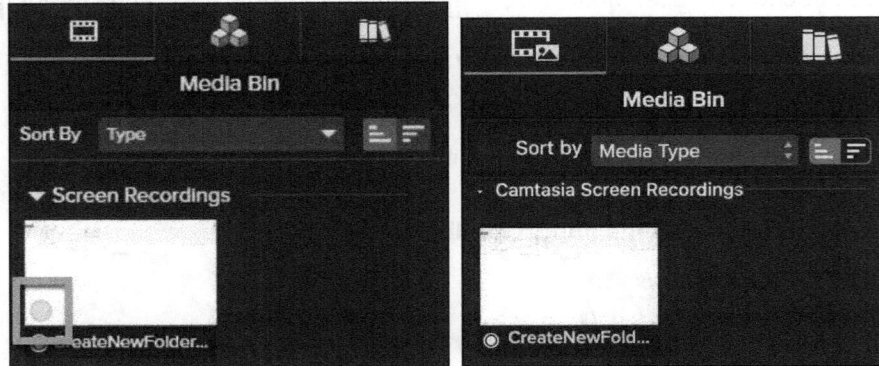

2. Delete and create a video proxy.

   ❑ if there is a proxy icon on the Media Bin video thumbnail, right click the video and choose **Proxy Video > Delete Proxy Video**

   The proxy icon is removed from the Media Bin video. Notice that deleting the proxy video **does not delete the media** from the Media Bin.

   ❑ if there isn't a proxy icon on the Media Bin asset, right click the video and choose **Proxy Video > Create Proxy Video**

3. If necessary, delete the proxy video.

   Next, you'll add the video media to the Timeline and the Canvas.

Guided Activity 14: Add Media to the Timeline and the Canvas

1. Add a video to the Timeline.

   ☐ on the **Media Bin**, right-click the video you just imported

   ☐ choose **Add to Timeline at Playhead**

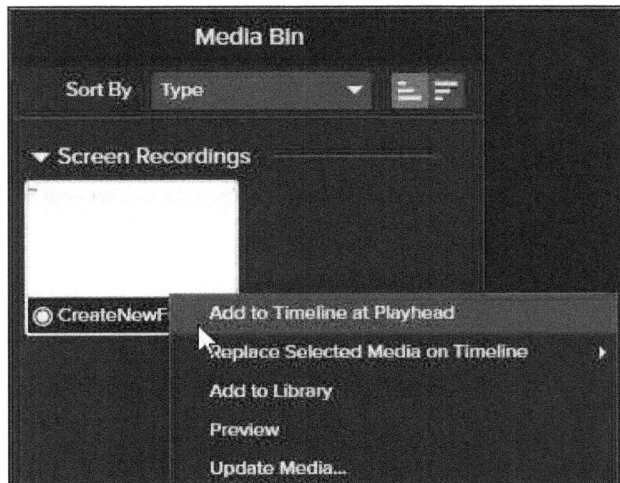

The video appears in two Camtasia locations: the Canvas and the Timeline. On the Timeline, the video is represented by a horizontal bar.

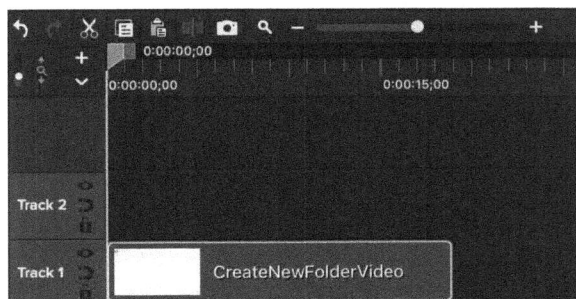

2. Preview a project on the Canvas.

   ☐ on the **Canvas**, click the **Play** button

As the video plays on the Canvas, notice the **Playhead** moving across the Timeline. You will work with the Playhead soon.

NOTES

3. Save the project.

  ☐ choose **File > Save**

  ☐ open **Camtasia 2025 Book Assets** > **Projects**

  ☐ name the Camtasia project **CreateNewFolder**

  ☐ from the bottom of the dialog box, ensure that **Create standalone project** is selected

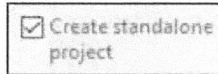

☑ Create standalone project

As mentioned during the last module, the **Create standalone project** option bundles all of the imported Media Bin assets together with the project file. This feature ensures that anyone opening the project file with Camtasia 2025 or newer will have all necessary assets to open and edit the project.

  ☐ click the **Save** button

PC users, you'll be alerted about opening the project file to make edits moving forward. Click the **OK** button.

Camtasia Project Files   ✕

Camtasia project saved.

To continue editing this video project, open the .tscproj file.

Learn more about Camtasia file types.

☐ Don't show again   **OK**

Depending upon your platform, saved projects get a slightly different file name extension. On the PC, files get a **tscproj** extension. Mac projects get a **cmproj** extension.

TechSmith Camtasia - CreateNewFolder.tscproj   46%   **CreateNewFolder.cmproj**   31%

Video Confidence Check

1. Ensure that the **CreateNewFolder** project is open and that you have completed all previous activities in this module.

2. On the **Timeline**, right-click the video you just added and choose **Delete**.

   While video has been removed from the Timeline, it is still in the Media Bin and can easily be added back onto the Timeline.

3. Ensure the **Playhead** is positioned at the far left of the Timeline.

4. **Right-click** the **video** in the **Media Bin** and choose **Add to Timeline at Playhead** to add the video back to the Timeline.

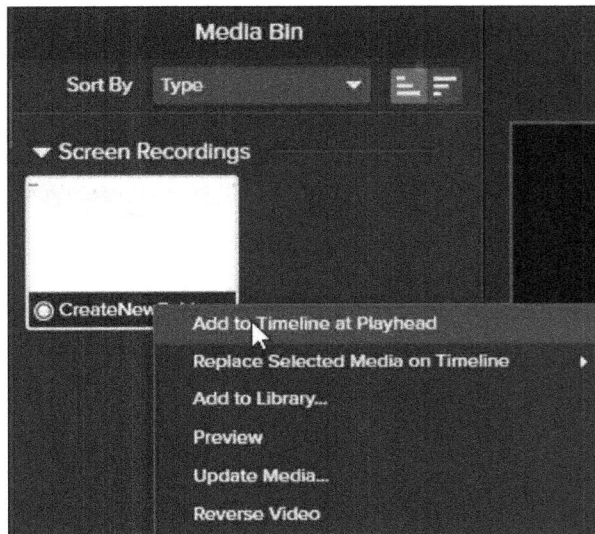

5. **Zoom closer** to the media in Track 1 by clicking the **Zoom timeline in** icon (the icon is located at the left of the Timeline).

   The ability to Zoom closer to Timeline objects will prove useful later when you need to split the audio or synchronize the video with other Timeline objects. You can always use the **Zoom timeline out** tool to move farther away from the Timeline or drag the slider (the circle between the plus and minus signs).

6. Save the project.

NOTES

NOTES

Adding Images

Camtasia supports many standard graphic formats, including BMP, GIF, and JPEG. If you don't have access to your own photographs or other assets, I've had great success with sites like BigStockPhoto, iStockPhoto, and Shutterstock. These websites offer extensive collections of inexpensive, royalty-free assets.

You'll find downloadable content in the Media area, Camtasia Assets or by visiting https://library.techsmith.com. While some TechSmith Library assets are free to use, most require an annual subscription.

Camtasia also includes a Library in the Media area containing several free assets you can use in your projects. You'll explore the Library soon.

Guided Activity 15: Import Images to the Media Bin

1. Open an existing Camtasia project.

   ☐ choose **File > Open Project**

   ☐ from the **Camtasia 2025 Book Assets > Projects** folder, open the **ImageMe** Camtasia project (from within the **ImageMe** folder)

As mentioned earlier, this book was written based on an early release of Camtasia 2025. Since the book's assets and project files were created, TechSmith has likely released multiple updates to the software. If you see the upgrade message shown below, click **Yes**, then click **OK** on the two upgrade alert messages to continue.

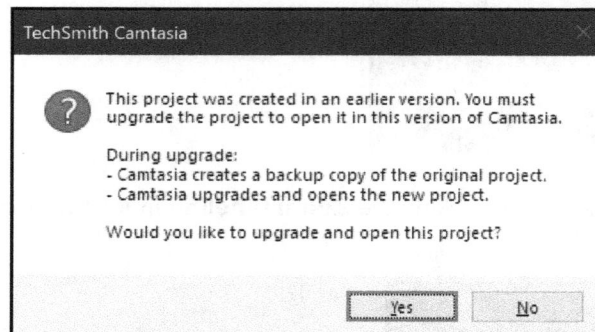

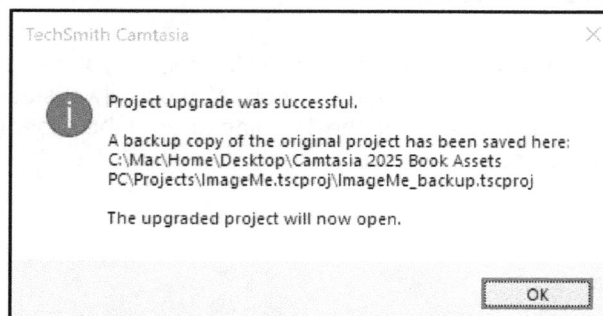

This project is identical to the one you were just working on. It has the CreateNewFolderVideo in the Media Bin and on the Timeline.

Next, you'll add multiple images to the Media Bin and then the Timeline.

2. Import an image to the Media Bin.

   ☐ choose **File > Import > Media**

   ☐ from the **Camtasia 2025 Book Assets** folder, open the **Image Files** folder

   ☐ select **logo.png** and then click **Open** (PC) or **Import** (Mac)

   The logo image appears in the Media Bin.

3. Import another image.

   ☐ choose **File > Import > Media**

   ☐ from the **Image Files** folder, open/import **mainart.jpg**

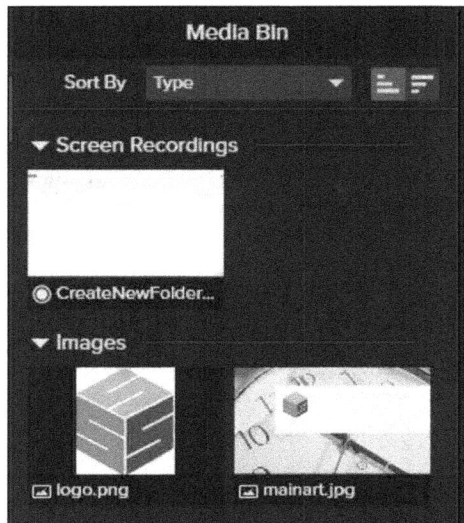

NOTES

Timeline Confidence Check

1. On the **Timeline**, drag the **CreateNewFolder** media to the **right** several seconds to leave space at the left for the **mainart** image. (You'll need at least 5 seconds of space to the left of the video media.)

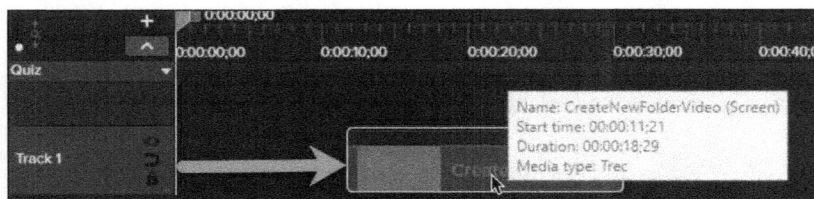

2. From the **Media Bin**, drag the **mainart** image to the beginning of Track 1 on the Timeline.

3. On the Timeline, there is likely a gap between the mainart object and the CreateNewFolder object.

   There are two ways you can remove the gap: 1) Drag the **CreateNewFolder** object **left** until it bumps up against the mainart image (as shown in the first image below). 2) Click the **Enable magnetic track** icon (as shown in the second image below)

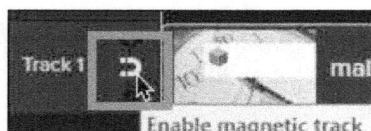

4. On the **Canvas**, click the **Play** button to preview the project.

   On the Canvas, you'll notice that the mainart image appears, disappears after a few seconds, and is then replaced by the video demonstrating how to create a new folder.

   If you want Timeline objects to appear one after the other, you've just learned how easy it is—simply drag or stretch objects left or right on the Timeline to control their timing and duration.

   If you want multiple Timeline items to appear on the Canvas at the same time, you'll need multiple Timeline tracks—something you'll learn about next.

5. Save the project.

Multi-Track Projects

You've added two assets to the Timeline: a video and an image. Both media objects appear on a single Timeline track called Track 1. You can easily add additional tracks to the Timeline. With multiple tracks, you gain precise control over when each object appears on the Canvas and how they relate to one another. For example, you could add your corporate logo to a new track above the video track to create a watermark effect—perfect for corporate branding.

Guided Activity 16: Add a Track

1. Ensure that the **ImageMe** project is open and that you have completed all the activities in this module up to this point

2. Insert a new track.

   ☐ on the top left of the Timeline, click **Add a track**

   On the Timeline, notice that **Track 2** has been added just above Track 1. Because Track 2 is above Track 1 on the Timeline, anything you add to Track 2 appears to float (stacked) above anything on Track 1 when viewed on the Canvas.

   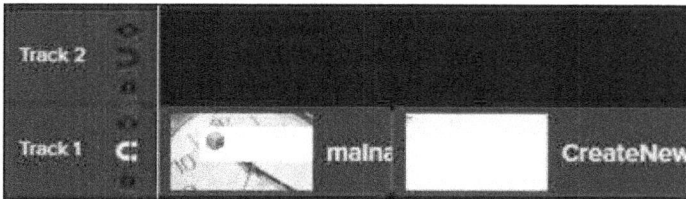

3. Add an image to Track 2.

   ☐ if necessary, drag the **Playhead** left to the **beginning** of the Timeline

   ☐ on the **Media Bin**, right-click the **logo** image and choose **Add to Timeline at Playhead**

   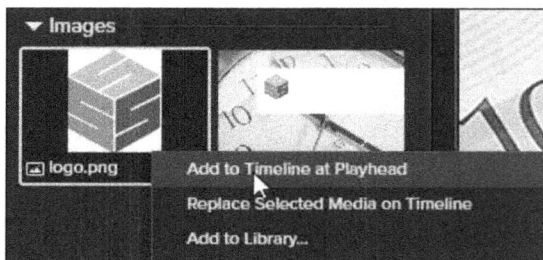

NOTES

Only one object can occupy a track at a given point in time on the Timeline. Because the Playhead was positioned at the 0:00 mark—and there was already an object on Track 1 at that time—the logo was automatically added to the next available track (in this case, the beginning of Track 2). If you hadn't manually added the second track before placing the image on the Timeline, Camtasia would have created the new track for you automatically.

4. Change when the logo appears on the Timeline.

    ☐ on **Track 2** of the Timeline, position your mouse pointer in the **middle** of the **logo** media object

    ☐ **drag** the logo media **right** until its **left edge** lines up with the left edge of the **CreateNewFolder** media on Track 1

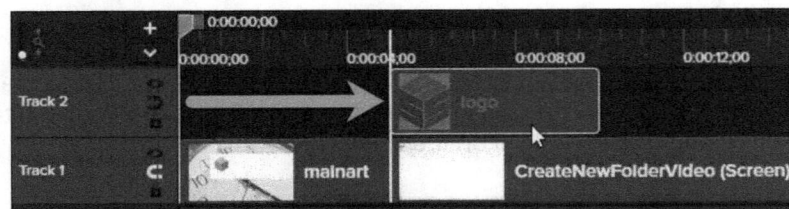

5. Position the Playhead and preview a portion of the video.

    ☐ on the **Timeline**, double-click the **CreateNewFolder** media

    The Playhead, which indicates a specific points in time, should now be positioned with the **CreateNewFolderVideo** and **logo** media objects.

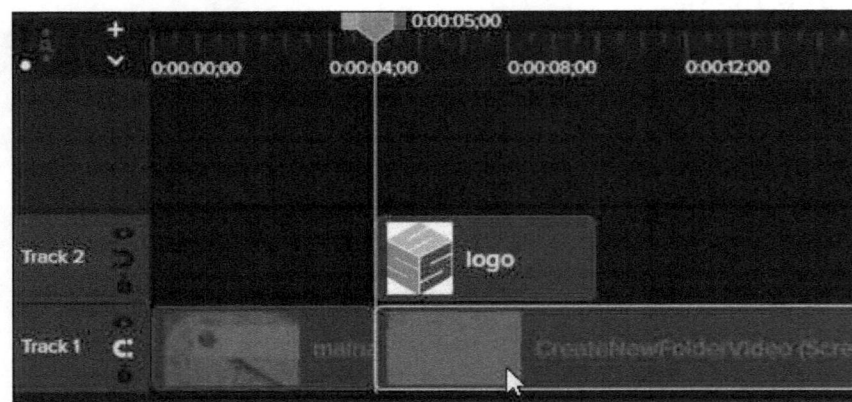

    ☐ on your keyboard, press [**spacebar**] to start previewing the video from the current Playhead position

    On the Canvas, notice that the logo image appears above the video and then disappears after a few seconds—long before the video finishes. You will edit the timing of the two media objects next.

6. Use the Timeline to extend the play time for the logo.

□ on the **Timeline**, use your mouse to **point** to the **right edge** of the logo object

□ when the mouse pointer changes to a **double-headed arrow**, stretch the **right** edge of the logo object **right** until the logo's object bar aligns when the video ends

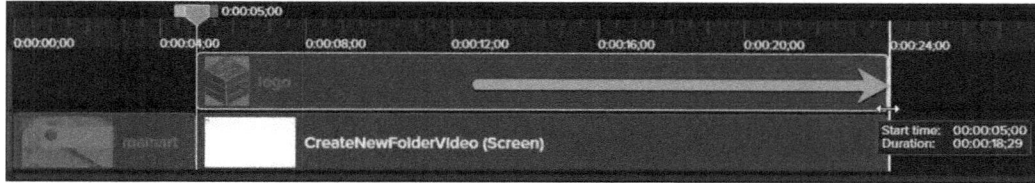

Note: If you are too close or too far away from the Timeline, working with Timeline objects can be challenging. Consider zooming closer to the Timeline as appropriate prior to manipulating with Timeline objects.

7. Preview the timing changes.

□ on the Timeline, double-click the **CreateNewFolder** video object

On the Timeline, the Playhead should once again be aligned with the **CreateNewFolder** object on the Timeline.

□ on your keyboard, press [**spacebar**] to Preview the project

On the Canvas, notice that the logo image is visible for the duration of the video. However, the logo is too big, and it doesn't look good positioned in the middle of the Canvas. You will fix both issues next.

□ on your keyboard, press [**spacebar**] again to stop the video preview

8. Save the project.

NOTES

NOTES

Guided Activity 17: Edit Media Properties

1. Ensure that the **ImageMe** project is open and that you have completed all the activities in this module up to this point

2. Display the Properties panel.

   ☐ on **Track 2,** right-click the **logo** and choose **Show Properties** (if you see **Hide Properties** in the menu instead of Show Properties, move to the next step)

   The Properties panel is located at the right side of the Camtasia window.

3. Use the Properties panel to make the logo smaller.

   ☐ near the top of the **Properties** panel, drag the **Scale** slider **left** to change the Scale to **50%** (if you find it difficult to get to exactly 50, type **50** into the Scale field at the right)

4. Lower the opacity of the logo.

   ☐ on the **Properties** panel, drag the **Opacity** slider **left** to change the Opacity to **40%** (again, if you find it difficult to get to exactly 40, type **40** into the field at the right)

5. Disable Canvas Snapping.

   ☐ choose **View** and disable **Enable Canvas Snapping** (ensure there is **not** a check mark next to the menu item)

   Disabling Canvas Snapping allows you to position objects on the Canvas more freely. When this option is enabled, objects tend to snap to the edges of the Canvas or to nearby media elements.

6. Change the logo's Canvas position.

   ☐ from above the **Canvas**, click the **Edit** mode icon

   ☐ on the Canvas, drag the logo near the **bottom right** of the video on the Canvas

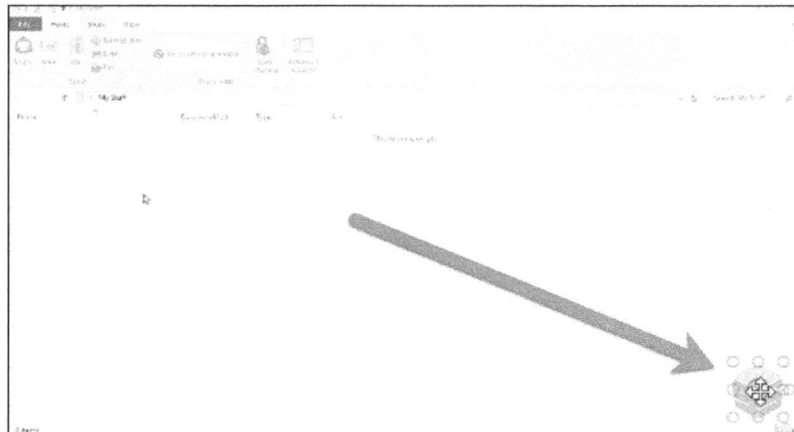

7. Save the project.

Cursor Effects

Earlier in this module, you added a video to the project demonstrating the process of creating a new folder on a computer (page 45). You've previewed that video several times during this module, so it's likely that you have already noticed the animated cursor. As the cursor moves, there are no click sounds or visual effects to draw the learner's attention to the clicks. Because the video was created with the Camtasia Recorder, the cursor can be enhanced with visual effects, click sounds, and more.

Guided Activity 18: Add Cursor Effects

1. Open and upgrade an existing project.

   ☐ using Camtasia, choose **File > Open Project**

   ☐ from **Camtasia 2025 Book Assets > Projects**, open the **MouseMe** folder

   ☐ open the **MouseMe** project

   ☐ when prompted, click **Yes** and then **OK** to upgrade the project

2. Preview the video.

   ☐ on the **Timeline**, double-click the **CreateNewFolder** media object to move the Playhead to the beginning of the media

   ☐ on your keyboard, press [**spacebar**] to preview the video

   As the video plays, notice the mouse cursor. The more cluttered the background, the harder the cursor may be for learners to see. During the steps that follow, you'll add a visual effect to make the cursor more noticeable onscreen.

3. Add a Cursor Highlight effect to the cursor in the video.

   ☐ on the **Timeline**, ensure that the **CreateNewFolderVideo** media is selected

   ☐ from the list of tools at the left, click **Cursor Effects**

   ☐ right-click the **Cursor Highlight** effect and choose **Add to Selected Media**

   On the **Timeline**, the effect is added to the selected media. You can see the video effects (and delete them) via the Effects arrow beneath the video object on the Timeline.

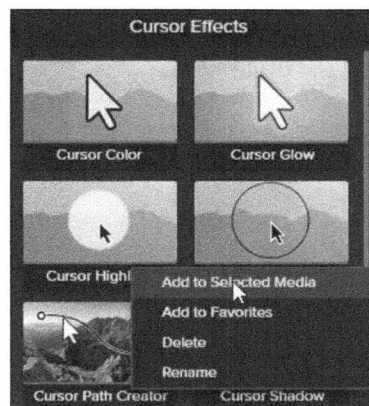

NOTES

4. Preview the cursor effect.

   ☐ on the **Timeline**, double-click the **CreateNewFolder** media to move the Playhead to the beginning of the video

   ☐ on your keyboard, press [**spacebar**]

   The cursor now includes a highlight effect. *How cool is that?*

   ☐ on your keyboard, press [**spacebar**] again to stop the Playhead and the preview

5. Change the Properties of the Cursor Effect.

   ☐ on the **Timeline**, right-click the **video media** and choose **Show Properties**

   Note: If the menu item says **Hide Properties**, the Properties panel is already open at the right of the Camtasia window.

   ☐ at the top of the Properties panel, click the **Cursor Properties** icon

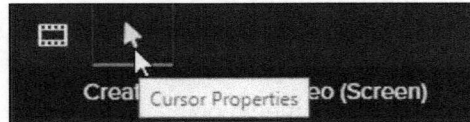

   ☐ on the **Properties** panel, **Cursor Highlight** area, **Color** section, select any color
   ☐ from the **Opacity** area, change the Opacity to **30%**
   ☐ from the **Size** area, drag the slider left to **30**

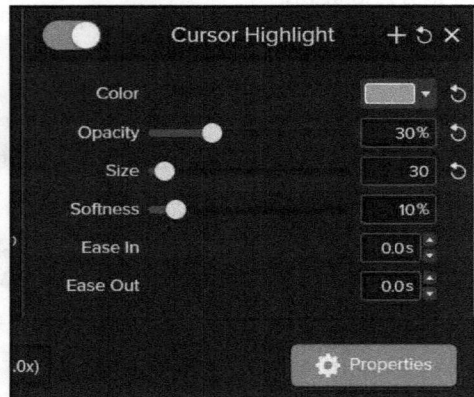

6. Preview the project.

   The highlight's color, size, and opacity should reflect your Property changes.

Cursor Effects Confidence Check

1. On the Timeline, just below the video media, click **Show effects**.

2. With the effects showing, right-click the **Cursor Highlight** effect and choose **Delete** (**Remove Effect** on the Mac) to delete it.

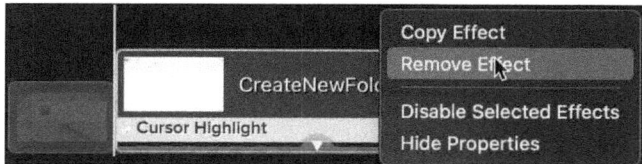

   Note: It's easy to accidentally delete Timeline media instead of a media effect. When deleting an effect, ensure that you right-click the effect, not the media itself.

3. Spend a few moments adding different **Cursor** effects to the video's cursor.

4. Spend a few moments adding **Left Click** effects to the video's cursor.

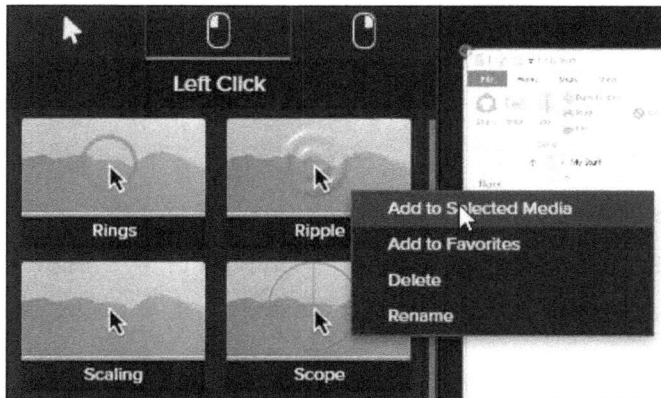

5. PC users, Save the project.
   Mac users, save and close all open projects.

NOTES

Cursor Editing

You have already learned that you can add cursor effects to imported TREC videos created with the Camtasia Recorder. However, the ability to add cursor effects is not limited to adding visual effects. If the size of your capture window is large and the recorded mouse pointer small, you can change the size of the cursor within Camtasia. If, during the recording process, you moved the mouse pointer down and to the right when you really wanted to move up and to the left, you'll appreciate Camtasia's ability to simplify the path or create a new path. And you can use the Elevate feature to ensure that the cursor always appears above other Canvas media.

Guided Activity 19: Smooth the Cursor Path

1. Create a new Camtasia project.

2. Change the Canvas size.

    ☐ PC users, choose **File > Project Settings**;
    Mac users, choose **Edit > Project Settings**

    ☐ from the **Canvas Dimensions** drop-down menu, choose **HD (1280x720)**

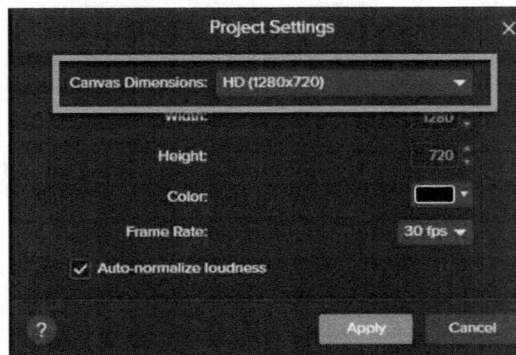

Project Settings	✕
Canvas Dimensions: HD (1280x720) ▼	
Width:	1280
Height:	720
Color:	■ ▼
Frame Rate:	30 fps ▼
✓ Auto-normalize loudness	
?	Apply Cancel

    ☐ click the **Apply** button

3. Import a video.

    ☐ choose **File > Import > Media**

    ☐ from **Camtasia 2025 Book Assets > Video Files**, open **SmoothMyCursor**

    ☐ if necessary, right-click the video and choose **Proxy Video > Delete Proxy Video**

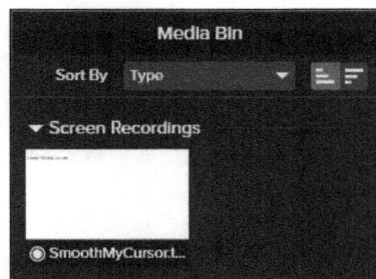

Media Bin		
Sort By Type ▼	☰ ☰	
▼ Screen Recordings		
◉ SmoothMyCursor.t...		

    Note: You can disable the automatic creation of proxy videos by choosing **Edit > Preferences** (PC) or **Camtasia > Settings** (Mac). On the **Advanced** tab (PC) or

General tab (Mac), remove the check mark from **Automatically create proxy media to improve editing performance**.

4. Add the imported video to the timeline.

   ☐ on the **Media Bin**, right-click the video and choose **Add to Timeline at Playhead**

5. Save the project to the **Camtasia 2025 Book Assets** folder as **Edited Cursor**.

6. Use the Canvas to play (preview) the video.

   Notice the size of the cursor and the strange, looping cursor path.

7. Smooth the cursor path.

   ☐ on the **Timeline**, ensure that the **SmoothMyCursor** media is selected

   ☐ from the list of tools at the left, click **Cursor Effects**

   ☐ from the top of Cursor Effects, ensure the first category is selected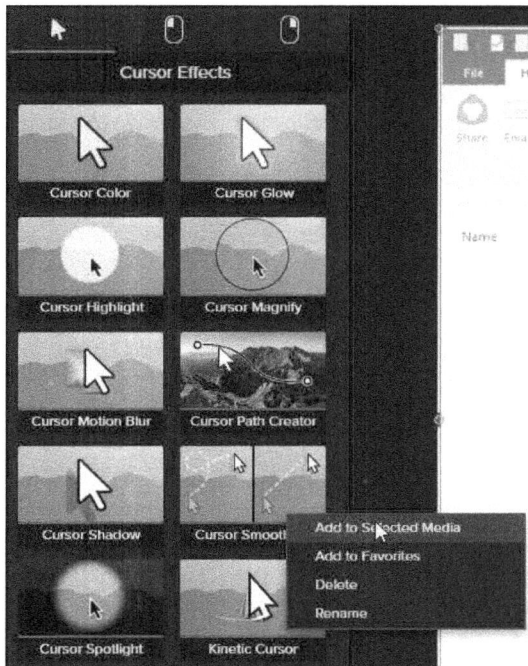

   ☐ right-click **Cursor Smoothing** and choose **Apply to Selected Media**

On the Timeline, notice that the Cursor Smooth effect has been added to the media.

NOTES

8. Use the Canvas to preview the video from the beginning.

   The path is smoother. However, the mouse sputters as it moves from point A to B to C.

9. Remove cursor pauses.

   ☐ on the **Timeline**, ensure that the **SmoothMyCursor** media is selected

   ☐ on the **Properties** panel, **Cursor Smoothing** area, deselect **Detect Cursor Pauses** (remove the checkmark)

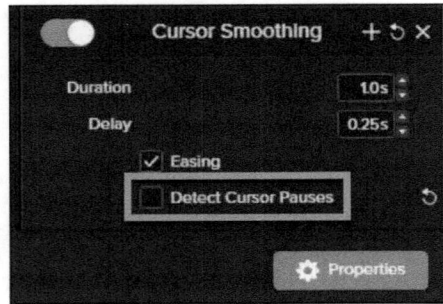

10. Use the Canvas to preview the video from the beginning.

    The cursor movement is better. However, the delay at the beginning of the video is not necessary. Let's trim away the first part of the video.

11. Trim a portion of the video.

    ☐ on the **Timeline**, observe the SmoothMyCursor media

    Each of the icons on the media represent potential cursor movement. Because of the smoothing effect, the first part of the video is not needed.

    ☐ on the **Timeline**, position the **Playhead** at the **beginning** of the video media

    ☐ on the **Playhead**, drag the **red** icon **right** to before the second mouse movement icon

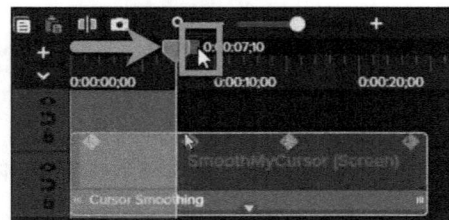

    ☐ on the **Timeline**, click the **cut** icon ✂

12. Preview the video from the beginning.

    Now that you've trimmed the beginning of the video, the cursor appears sooner—but its position on the Canvas has changed. It's now immediately positioned over the Format menu. If you want full control over the cursor's movement and positioning, you'll need to edit the cursor path.

13. Remove the media from the Timeline.

    ❑ on the **Timeline**, right-click the **SmoothMyCursor** media and choose **Delete**

    As you've seen previously, removing media from the Timeline does not delete the media from the project—the video is still in the Media Bin.

14. Save the project.

NOTES

NOTES

Guided Activity 20: Edit the Cursor Path

1. Ensure that the **Edited Cursor** project you created during the previous activity is still open and that the **SmoothMyCursor** video has been imported into the Media Bin.

2. Add a Media Bin asset to the Timeline.

   ☐ on the **Timeline**, position the Playhead back at the beginning

   ☐ on the **Media Bin**, right-click the imported video **SmoothMyCursor** and choose **Add to Timeline at Playhead**

3. Preview the video from the beginning.

   The cursor path is not very smooth. You have already learned that you can quickly smooth out the cursor path. However, for complete control over the cursor, you need to edit the cursor path.

4. Edit the cursor path.

   ☐ on the **Timeline**, select the video media

   ☐ on the **Properties** panel, click the **Cursor Properties** icon

   ☐ on the **Properties** panel, click the **Edit Cursor Path** button

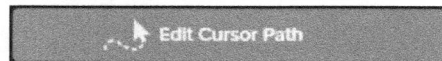

   The Edit Cursor Path options open.

   ☐ from the **Option** drop-down menu, ensure **Simplify Existing Path** is selected

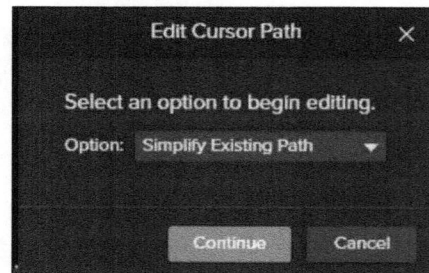

   ☐ click the **Continue** button

5. Move the Playhead to see the cursor points.

   ❏ on the **Timeline**, drag the **Playhead** right and then left a few times

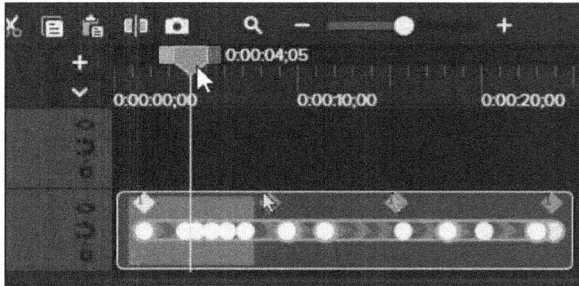

   On the Canvas, you can see editable cursor points.

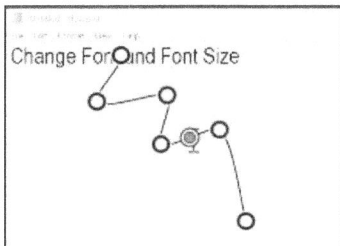

6. Delete a cursor point.

   ❏ on the **Timeline**, move the Playhead to **3;28**

   ❏ on the **Canvas**, select the cursor point shown in the box below

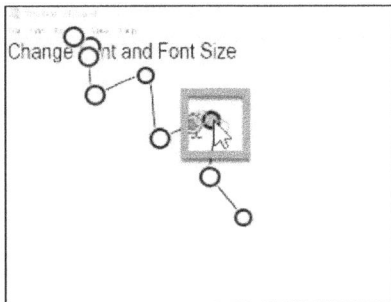

   ❏ **right-click** the cursor point and choose **Delete Cursor Point**

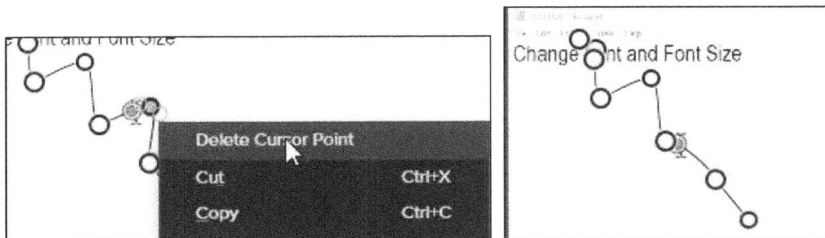

NOTES

7. Move a cursor point.

❐ on the **Canvas**, select the cursor point shown in the box below

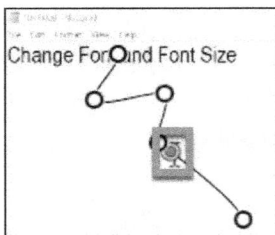

❐ **drag** the cursor down and to the right until it is centered between the cursor points

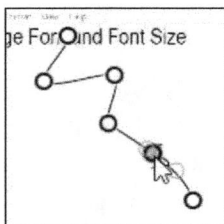

Cursor Paths Confidence Check

1. Continue to edit the mouse path at the beginning of the video similar to the path shown in the image below.

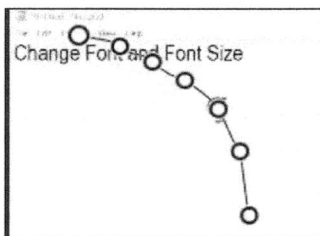

2. Preview the video from the beginning.

   Notice that the edited path is no longer ragged like it was before. However, there is a delay between each of the cursor points and the cursor movement is not very smooth. There are two ways to address the delays. You can add cursor points or use the Timeline to close up the delay between points.

3. On the Canvas, right-click between two points and choose **Add Cursor Point**.

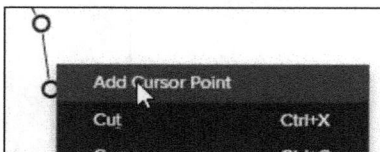

4. Continue adding a few more cursor points along the cursor path.

5. Preview the video and notice that the cursor path is now even smoother.

6. On the Timeline, zoom closer to the video media.

   The cursor points are shown as the white dots along the Timeline. The gaps between the cursor points represent the delays.

7. Drag some of the highlighted cursor point left to remove gaps between the points.

8. Preview the video and notice that the speed of the mouse motion is better and better.

9. Spend a few moments removing the delay between additional cursor points.

10. When satisfied with the path and the timing, click the **Finish Editing** button on the Properties panel.

   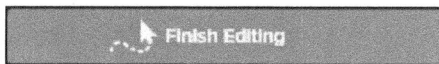

   Note: You can restore the original cursor path by clicking the **Restore Path** button.

NOTES

Guided Activity 21: Control the Cursor Image, Size, and Elevation

1. Ensure that the Edited Cursor project you created during the previous activity is still open.

2. Change the appearance of the cursor.

   ☐ on the **Timeline**, select the video media

   ☐ on the **Properties** panel, click the **Cursor Properties** icon

   ☐ from the **Cursor** area, click the drop-down

   ☐ from the drop-down menu beneath that, choose **Windows Cursors** or **Mac Cursors**

   ☐ select any cursor you like

3. Change the size of the cursor.

   ☐ on the **Properties** panel, drag the **Scale** slider **left** or **right** to resize the cursor as you see fit

4. Change the cursor elevation.

   ☐ on the **Properties** panel, **Elevation** drop-down menu, choose **Always on Top**

   The elevation feature brings the cursor above other screen elements, ensuring that it is always visible.

5. Preview the video to see the results. (Because there aren't media objects on the canvas to conflict with the cursor, the only effect you won't see in action is the elevation feature.)

6. Save the project. (Mac users, close the project.)

iCONLOGiC™

Module 4: Groups, Annotations, and Animation

In This Module You Will Learn About:

And You Will Learn To:

Groups

Changing the timing of media objects on the Timeline is easy—drag Timeline objects left or right to adjust when they appear, or drag them up or down to move them between Timeline tracks. However, moving objects individually can disrupt Timeline synchronization with other media on different tracks. For example, there is an image positioned on a track that is meant to appear on the Canvas at the same time as a video on another track. If you move the image left or right but forget to move the video, the timing synchronization between the two Timeline object is lost.

Because coordinating media across multiple tracks can become complex, Camtasia's grouping feature is especially helpful. Instead of moving objects one at a time, you can group multiple items—even across different tracks—and move them together as a single unit.

Guided Activity 22: Create a Group

1. Using Camtasia, open the **AnnotateMe** project from **Camtasia 2025 Book Assets > Projects**. (When prompted, click **Yes** and then **OK** to upgrade the project.)

2. Move a Timeline object.

   ☐ on the **Timeline**, drag the **logo** media to the **right** by a few seconds

   After moving the logo, notice that the CreateNewFolderVideo object did not move. Since these two objects are meant to appear onscreen together, it would be better to group them before moving either one.

3. Undo the last step.

   ☐ choose **Edit > Undo**

   The logo should now be back in its original Timeline position.

4. Create a group.

   ☐ on the **Timeline**, select the **CreateNewFolderVideo** media in Track **1**

   ☐ press [**shift**] and select the **logo** in Track **2** (then release [**shift**])

   Both the video and the logo should now be selected.

   ☐ choose **Edit > Group**

   The selected objects are now grouped. The logo, which was in Track 2, has been moved into the new group on Track 1

Note:
To Ungroup, right-click a group and choose **Ungroup**.

Note: If you double-click a group, the group opens so that objects within the group can be edited or replaced. To close an open group, click the close group icon on the Timeline.

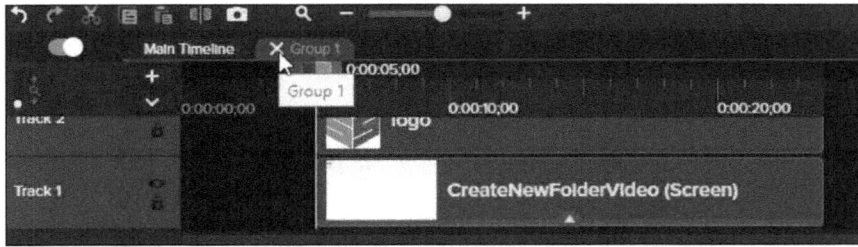

5. Rename a group.

   ☐ on the **Timeline**, right-click the group in Track **1** and choose **Rename Group**

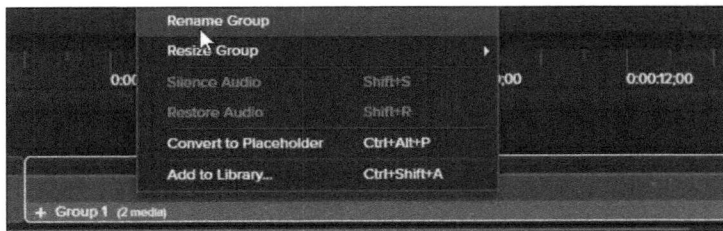

   The group's default name, Group 1, is selected.

   ☐ change the group's name to **Creating Folders** and press [**enter**]

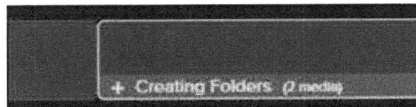

6. Move Timeline objects as a group.

   ☐ on the **Timeline**, position the Playhead at the 30 second mark

   ☐ on the **Timeline**, drag the **Creating Folders** group **right** until its left edge lines up with the **Playhead** (the 30 second mark on the Timeline)

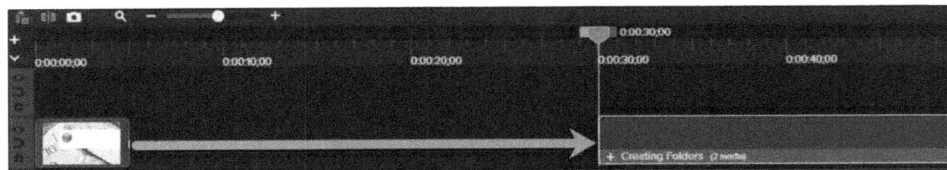

   Both objects in the group move, leaving a sizable gap between the mainart object and the Creating Folders group. You'll be adding media within the gap soon.

7. Remove an empty track.

   ☐ at the left of the Timeline, right-click the words **Track 2** and choose **Remove All Empty Tracks**

   Note: Empty tracks do no harm, and it is never a requirement to remove them.

NOTES

Annotations

A Camtasia annotation is a visual element that you can add to the Timeline or Canvas. They draw attention, provide instruction, or enhance viewer understanding. Annotations are part of Camtasia's toolbox for making your videos more engaging and easier to follow. There are several types of Annotations, including **Callouts** (shapes that can contain text), Arrows, Lines, Shapes, Motions, and Keystrokes.

In the Demo project you opened at the beginning of this book, several callouts are already synchronized with the voiceover narration. One of those callouts is shown in the image below—it contains the words *CREATE* and *FOLDERS*. In the following activities, you'll add and format a few callouts of your own.

Guided Activity 23: Add a Callout

1. Ensure that the **AnnotateMe** project is open and that you have completed all previous activities in this module.

2. Insert a callout.

   ☐ on the **Timeline**, double-click the **mainart** image to move the Playhead to the **far left** of the Timeline

   ☐ from the list of tools at the left, click **Annotations** [Annotations]

   ☐ on the **Annotations** panel, click **Callouts** (the first Annotation type) [icon]

   ☐ from the **Style** drop-down menu, choose **Basic**

   ☐ right-click the **white rectangle with the black text** and choose **Add to Timeline at Playhead**

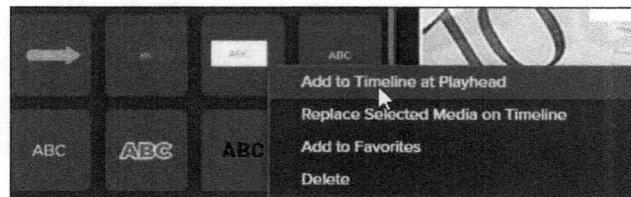

Because the Playhead was positioned at 00:00 on the Timeline, and media was already present on Track 1 at that point, a new track was added to accommodate the caption.

3. Remove a callout's border.

☐ ensure that the new annotation is selected

☐ at the top of the **Properties** panel, click the **Annotation Properties** icon

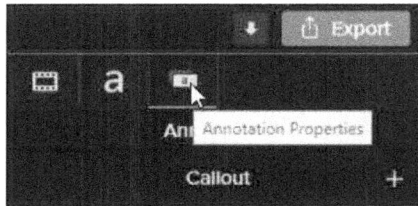

☐ on the callout **Properties** panel, change the **Thickness** to **0** (you can either type a **0** into the text field or drag the slider as far **left** as it will go)

4. Format the callout's text.

☐ with the annotation still selected, at the top of the **Properties** panel, click **Text Properties**

☐ change the Font to **Verdana (Regular)**

☐ change the Color to **Black**

☐ change the Size to **80**

☐ change the Alignment to **Left**

☐ deselect **Auto-resize Text**

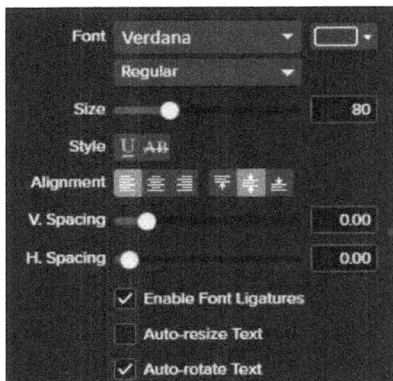

If Auto-resize Text is selected, the text will automatically shrink to fit within the text box as you type. By deselecting Auto-resize Text, you ensure that the font size in this Annotation remains fixed at 80 points, regardless of how much text you enter.

NOTES

NOTES

5. Add the callout text.

☐ replace the existing text in the callout with the words **CREATE FOLDERS**

☐ resize and position the callout similar to the image below

6. Save the project.

Themes

Many organizations require consistent use of fonts and colors across projects. Similar to Style Sheets and Object Styles in other development tools and word processors you've likely used, Themes can contain several formatting options. Once you've created and set up a Theme, you can quickly apply the Theme to selected Timeline objects to ensure formatting consistency.

Guided Activity 24: Apply and Create Themes

1. Ensure that the **AnnotateMe** project is open and that you have completed all previous activities in this module.

2. Add a second callout to the Timeline.

   ☐ on the **Timeline**, double-click the **mainart** image to move the Playhead to the **far left** of the Timeline

   ☐ from the **Annotations** tools, click **Callouts**

   ☐ from the annotations **Style** drop-down menu, choose **Basic**

   ☐ right-click the **white rectangle with the black text** and choose **Add to Timeline at Playhead**

   The new callout is using the default formatting and does not match the appearance of your first callout.

3. Apply Themes to an object.

   ☐ with the newest callout selected on the Canvas, click either the **Text Properties** icon or **Annotation Properties** icon on the **Properties** panel

   ☐ on the **Properties** panel, **Theme** drop-down menu, choose **Default**

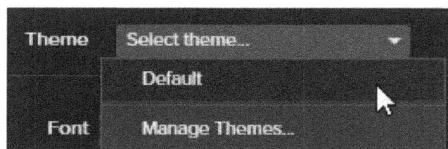

   The font formatting and background color of the selected callout change to reflect the properties of the Default Theme.

4. Create a new Theme.

   ☐ with the newest callout selected, click the **Theme** drop-down menu and choose **Manage Themes**

NOTES

The first time you select Manage Themes, you will see an alert. The alert, which gives a high-level overview of a theme, will not appear a second time.

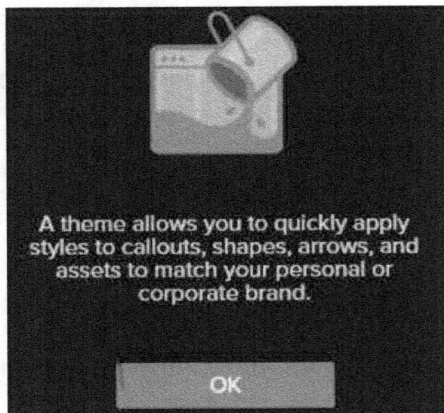

A theme allows you to quickly apply styles to callouts, shapes, arrows, and assets to match your personal or corporate brand.

OK

☐ click the **OK** button

The **Theme Manager** opens.

☐ click the **Create New Theme** icon (the **plus sign**)

Theme Manager ×

Theme | Algonquin Autumn | ⚙ ▾ | + | Preview background ☑

Colors   Fonts   Logo

The New Theme dialog box opens.

☐ name the new Theme **SuperSim Theme**

New Theme ×

Theme Name: | SuperSim Theme |

OK   Cancel

☐ click the **OK** button

The SuperSim theme opens and is ready for editing.

5. Set a Theme's Font.

   ☐ from within the **Theme Manager**, and with the **SuperSim Theme** selected, click the **Fonts** tab

   ☐ change **Font 1** to **Verdana**

6. Set a Theme's Colors.

   ☐ from within the **Theme Manager**, and with the **SuperSim Theme** selected, click the **Colors** tab

   ☐ change the **Foreground** color to **Black** (this controls the color of the text in the callout)

   ☐ change the **Background1** color to **White**

   ☐ change the **Annotation Background** to **Background1**

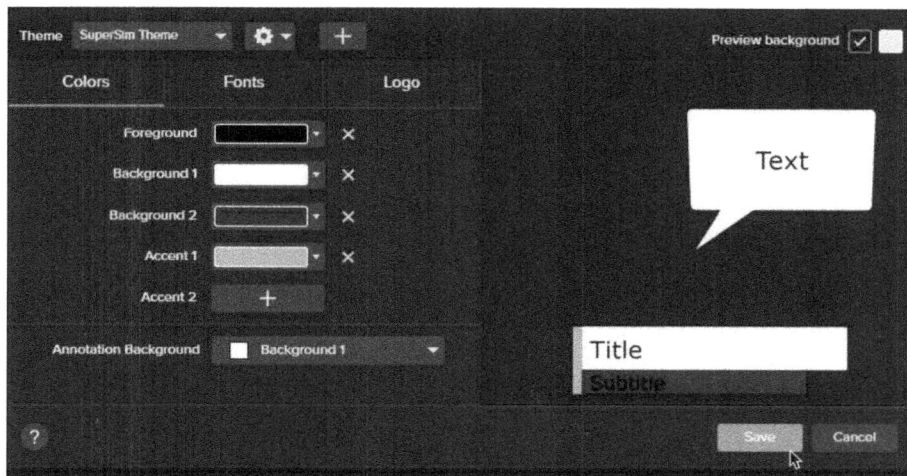

   ☐ click the **Save** button

7. Apply Themes to multiple callouts.

   ☐ select both of the callouts you've added to the Timeline so far (selecting one and [**shift**]-**clicking** the second one works great)

   ☐ from the **Themes** drop-down menu on the **Properties** panel, choose **Default**

   Both callouts take on the attributes of the Default Theme.

   ☐ with both callouts still selected, click the **Themes** drop-down menu and choose **SuperSim Theme**

NOTES

NOTES

Both annotations take on the attributes of the SuperSim Theme.

If you've used styles in other programs, the behavior of a Theme in Camtasia will be familiar to you. However, the formatting power of Camtasia Themes is somewhat limited. You cannot control many object properties, such as border thickness, color, or drop shadows, with a Theme.

Additionally, if you update a Theme, objects that use it do not automatically reflect the changes. You'll need to manually reselect the objects and reapply the Theme. Hopefully, as Camtasia continues to be updated by TechSmith, more advanced formatting options will be added to the Themes feature.

8. Delete just the second callout you added.

Guided Activity 25: Apply Image Color to Callout Text

1. Ensure that the **AnnotateMe** project is open and that you have completed all previous activities in this module.

2. Pick up color from an image and apply it to selected text.

   ☐ on the **Canvas**, double-click the callout and highlight the word **CREATE**.

   ☐ at the top of the **Properties** panel, click the **Text Properties** icon $\boxed{a}$

   ☐ from the **font color** drop-down menu, select the **eyedropper** icon

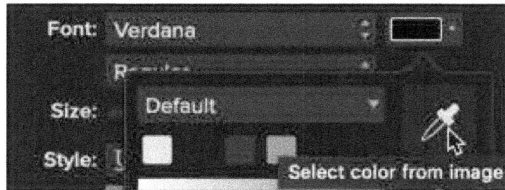

   ☐ using the **eyedropper**, click the green "**S**" on the logo

   The logo color you clicked with the **eyedropper** tool is applied to the highlighted text in the callout.

3. Save the project.

NOTES

NOTES

Callouts Confidence Check

1. Click in front of the word **FOLDERS** and press [**enter**].

2. Press [spacebar] a few times to indent the word **FOLDERS**.

CREATE

FOLDERS

3. On the **Timeline**, right-click the callout annotation and **Copy** it to the clipboard.

4. On the **Timeline**, position the **Playhead** just to the **right** of the callout.

5. PC users, right-click the existing callout and choose **Paste**.
   Mac users, right-click just to the right of the callout and choose **Paste Media at Playhead**

6. Drag the newest callout so it is positioned just after the first callout in Track 2.

7. Double-click the new callout and change the word **CREATE** to **RENAME**.

RENAME

FOLDERS

8. On the **Timeline**, position the Playhead just to the right of the second callout.

9. PC users, right-click the existing callout and choose **Paste**.
   Mac users, right-click just to the right of the callout and choose **Paste Media at Playhead**

10. Drag the newest callout so it is positioned just after the second callout in Track 2.

11. Drag the new callout up against the second callout.

12. Double-click the new callout and change the word **CREATE** to **DELETE**.

13. Change the word **FOLDERS** to **RESTORE**.

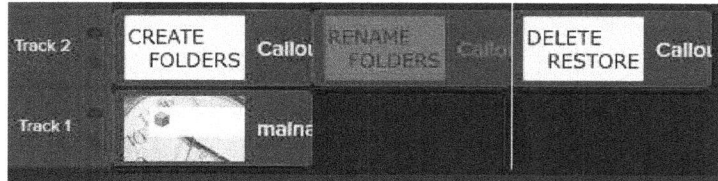

14. Save the project.

15. Create a **new** Camtasia project.

16. Spend a few moments adding some of the other Annotations to the project. (There is no need to save the new project so play as much as you'd like.)

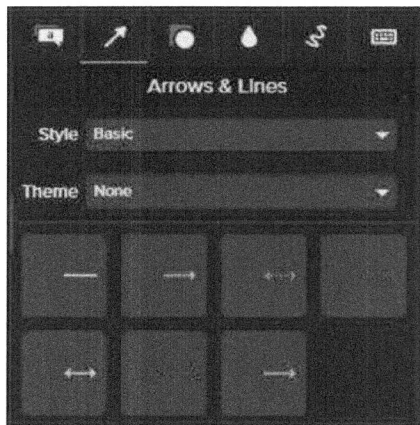

As you add the Annotations, notice the formatting options available to you on the Properties panel. You'll find that the options vary depending upon the type of Annotation you're working with.

17. Select any annotation and notice that there is a star in the upper right.

18. Click the star icon to turn it yellow and add the object as a **Favorite**.

19. From the tools at the left, click **Favorites** to see the shape that you've just added. From this point you can easily add the object to your Timeline or Canvas. (You can remove a Favorite by right-clicking and choosing **Remove Favorite**.)

   Note: Favorites added to one project will be available to all projects.

20. Mac users, you can close the project (there is no need to save when prompted). PC users, you'll be prompted to save the project when opening the next one. There is no need to save when prompted.

NOTES

Behaviors

Behaviors are animations designed to add visual appeal to your project. They can be applied to images, video clips, and various types of Annotations. A Behavior can be added to a single object or combined with other Behaviors to create unique effects.

Guided Activity 26: Add a Behavior to a Callout

1. Using Camtasia, open and upgrade the **BehaveMe** project from **Camtasia 2025 Book Assets > Projects**.

   This project has several callouts that have been added to Tracks 2 and 3. In particular, notice the three ampersands (**&**) added to Track 2 at **10;05**, **15;18**, and **20;18**.

   The stacking order of assets on the Timeline is important. Notice that each ampersand appears behind the callouts you added earlier. This stacking effect was easily achieved by placing the ampersand on a lower Timeline track.

   In the image above, the DELETE RESTORE callout is on Track 3, while the ampersand is on Track 2. Objects in higher tracks are positioned above those in lower tracks.

   In the next step, you'll add a Behavior to the ampersands.

2. Add a Behavior to a callout.

   ☐ on Track 2, double-click the first **ampersand** positioned at **10;05** on the **Timeline** to highlight object on both the Timeline and on the Canvas

   ☐ from the list of tools at the left, click **Behaviors**

   ☐ right-click **Jump And Fall** and choose **Add to Selected Media**

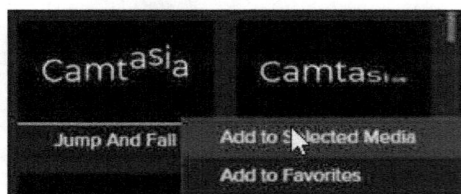

The Jump and Fall effect is applied to the callout and appears below the Timeline object in the Effects area. To remove an effect from an object, display the effects, right-click the effect, and choose **Delete** (PC) or **Remove Effect** (Mac).

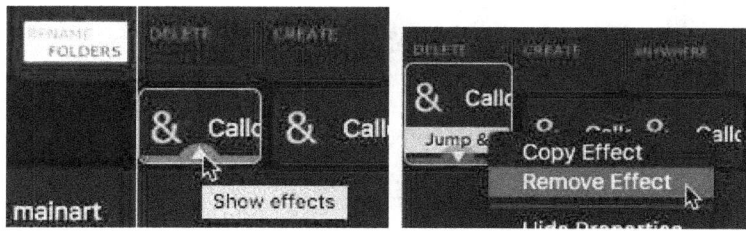

3. Preview the effect.

   ☐ on the **Timeline**, move the **Playhead** just to the left of the **ampersand** you just altered

   ☐ press [**spacebar**] on your keyboard **or** click the **Play** button on the Canvas

   When the Playhead reaches the **DELETE RESTORE** callout, the ampersand drops in from the top of the Canvas, bounces a few times, and then drops off the bottom. Next, you'll delay the appearance of the ampersand to enhance the effect.

4. Use the Timeline to delay the appearance of an object on the Canvas.

   ☐ on the **Timeline**, drag the **left edge** of the **ampersand** callout **right** a few seconds

5. Preview the timing change.

   ☐ on the **Timeline**, move the **Playhead** just to the left of the **RENAME FOLDERS** callout (the second callout on Track 2)

   ☐ press [**spacebar**] on your keyboard **or** click the **Play** button on the Canvas

   A few seconds after the DELETE RESTORE callout appears on the Canvas, the animated ampersand appears and performs its animation.

6. Modify the Properties of a Behavior.

   ☐ on Track 2, double-click the **ampersand** you've been working with (the first ampersand) to highlight it on the Canvas

   Currently, the ampersand drops in from the top of the Canvas. Let's explore some other effects you can apply to the callout.

   ☐ on the **Properties** panel, select **Behavior Properties**

The Jump & Fall effect has three tabs: **In**, **During**, and **Out**. The **In** tab controls the effect when the object first appears on the Canvas. The **During** tab defines the action while the object is on the Canvas. The **Out** tab determines the effect when the object leaves the Canvas.

NOTES

NOTES

☐ from the **Jump & Fall** Properties area, select the **In** tab

☐ from the **Style** drop-down menu, choose **Hinge**

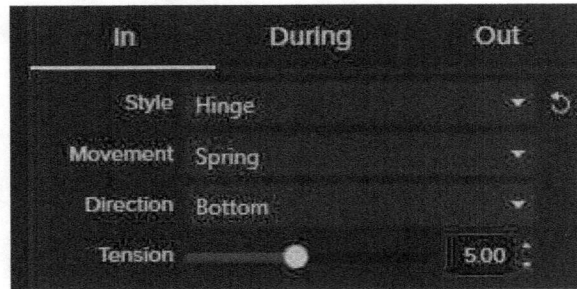

Behaviors Confidence Check

1. With the Playhead positioned just to the left of the **ampersand** you just altered, preview the effect on the Canvas.

   The ampersand should swing up from the bottom of the Canvas.

2. Spend a few moments playing with the **In**, **During**, and **Out** settings available on the **Properties** panel.

3. Add a Behavior to the remaining two ampersands (the ampersands are positioned on the **Timeline** at **15;18**, and **20;18**).

4. Preview the effects and adjust the timing of the ampersand callouts as you see fit.

5. Adjust the **In**, **During**, and **Out** properties of the effects as you see fit.

6. Select and then group mainart image and the callouts (name the group **Introduction to folders**).

7. Save the project. (Mac users, close the project.)

Transitions

You can use Transitions to add a smooth, professional visual break between any Timeline media. The Transitions panel offers various effect types, including arrows, wipes, blurs, and more. Once applied to media, you can control the duration of the transition and even reverse it.

Guided Activity 27: Add a Transition to a Group

1. Using Camtasia, open and upgrade the **TransitionMe** project from **Camtasia 2025 Book Assets** > **Projects**.

2. Add a Transition to selected media.

   ☐ from the tools at the left, click **Transitions**

   ☐ on the **Timeline**, select the **Get Ready** group

   ☐ on the **Transitions** panel, right-click the **Blob** transition and choose **Add to Selected Media**

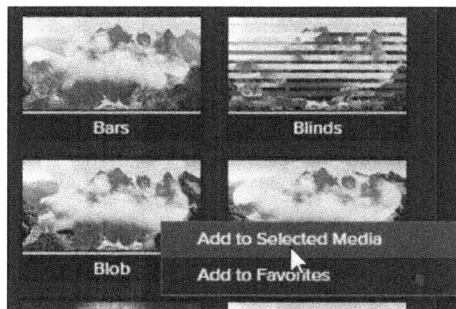

On the Timeline, the Blob transition has been added to the beginning of the selected group and also to the beginning of the next group. You can tell that a transition has been applied by the green rectangles. The transition was added to the second group (even though it wasn't selected) because, by default, transitions are applied to both the beginning and end of a selected group, as well as to the beginning of the next group it touches.

3. Save the project.

NOTES

Guided Activity 28: Modify Transition Timing

1. Ensure that the **TransitionMe** project is open.

2. Preview the project from the beginning.

   As the video plays on the Canvas, the Blob transition appears at the beginning and end of the first clip and again at the beginning of the second clip. It's a cool effect, but you'd like to speed it up.

3. Modify Transition Timing.

   ☐ on the **Timeline**, drag the **right edge** of the first green transition icon a bit to the **left**

   ☐ drag the **left** edge second green transition a bit to the **right**

4. Preview the project from the beginning.

   The timing for each transition should be a bit faster than before.

Transitions Confidence Check

1. Working in the **TransitionMe** project, add any transition(s) you like to each of the groups.

2. Preview the project to see the transitions.

3. Edit the speed of the transitions as you see fit.

4. Save the project.

Custom Animation

By now, you've seen that Camtasia is a powerhouse for recording screen actions, is flexible when adding media, and offers a wealth of built-in animations you can apply to Timeline objects, including, but not limited to, transitions and behaviors.

Let's kick things up a notch and create a custom animation. You're about to launch a rocket into the sky, fly it around, and land it back where it started. Move over, SpaceX!

Guided Activity 29: Create an Animation

1. Using Camtasia, open and upgrade the **LaunchMeLandMe** project from **Camtasia2022Data > Projects**.

2. Add a Custom Animation to Timeline media.

   ❑ on Track **3** of the **Timeline**, select the **Rocket** media

   ❑ from the list of tools at the left, select **Animations**

   Note: PC users, there are two tabs grouped with Animations: Zoom-n-Pan and Animations. Select the second tab, **Animations**.

   ❑ drag the **Custom** animation onto the **Rocket** media on the **Timeline** (don't drag the animation to the Canvas but to the Timeline media)

   An arrow appears on the Timeline to represent the animation. The left edge of the arrow, marked by the smaller circle, indicates the point where the animation begins. The right edge, marked by the larger circle, represents where the animation ends.

   ❑ drag the animation arrow until its **left edge** is aligned at **1;00**

   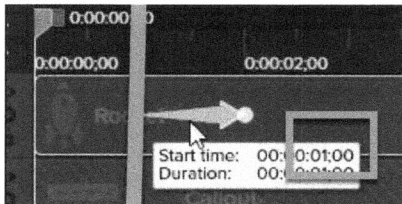

   ❑ on the animation arrow, select the larger circle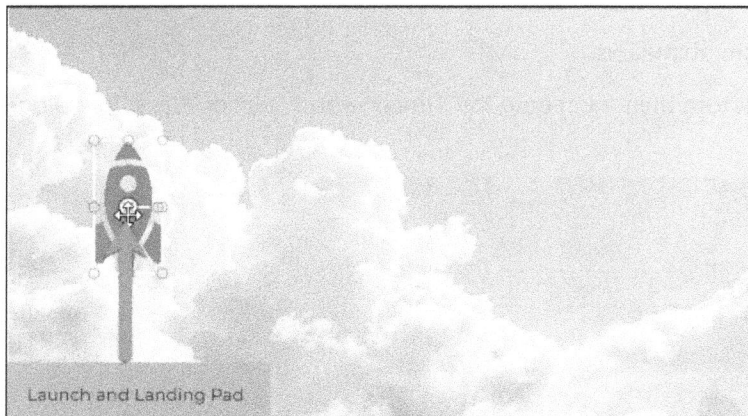
   ❑ on the **Canvas**, drag the rocket up into the clouds

NOTES

3. Drag the Playhead to the beginning of the Timeline and then preview the video.

   The rocket lifts off from the launch pad.

4. Add another Custom animation.

   ❏ drag a second Custom animation onto the Timeline and position it just to the **right** of the first one

   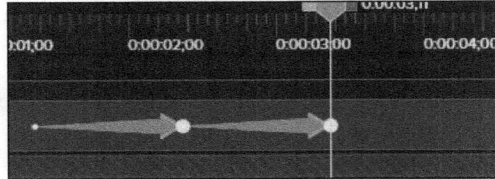

   ❏ on the **Timeline**, select the larger circle of the newest animation arrow

   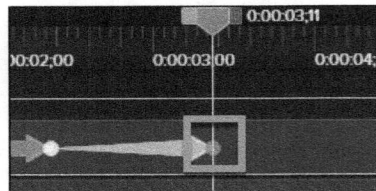

   ❏ on the **Canvas**, select the **Rotate** icon and rotate the rocket so that it is on its side

   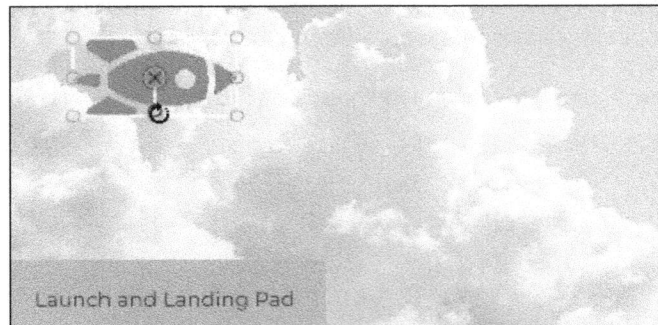

   Launch and Landing Pad

5. Drag the Playhead to the beginning of the Timeline and then preview the video.

   Notice that the rocket lifts off from the launchpad and then rotates to face right.

6. Add another Custom animation.

   ❏ drag a third **Custom** animation onto the Timeline and position it just to the right of the second one

   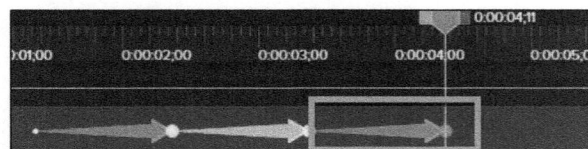

❑ on the **Timeline**, select the larger circle on the newest animation

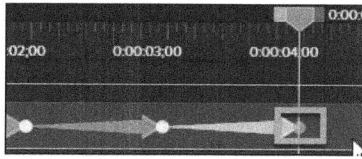

❑ on the **Canvas**, drag the rocket to the **right** side of the screen

7. Drag the Playhead to the beginning of the Timeline and then preview the video.

This time, the rocket lifts off from the launchpad, rotates, and then flies across the screen.

Animation Confidence Check

Your mission is to return the rocket safely to the launchpad.

1. Add more custom animations to the Timeline.

❑ one animation should turn the rocket back up into the sky

❑ one animation should turn the rocket back toward the left side of the screen

❑ one animation should rotate the rocket into the landing position

❑ one final animation should allow the rocket to land

2. Preview the animation.

3. Save the project.

NOTES

Corner Pin Mode

Using Corner Pin Mode, you can integrate media on the Canvas and create the illusion that the assets were created to work together. In the following activity, you'll add two assets to the Canvas: an image of a person using a tablet and a video demonstration. The two assets were never intended to be shown onscreen together because the angles in the image do not match the angles in the video. Using Corner Pin Mode, you will change the angles of the video so it works remarkably well with the image.

Guided Activity 30: Use Corner Pin Mode

1. Create a new Camtasia project.

2. Add media to the Media Bin and the Timeline.

   ☐ choose **File > Import > Media**

   ☐ from **Camtasia 2025 Book Assets > Image Files**, open **tablet.jpg**

   ☐ on the **Media Bin**, right-click the tablet image and choose **Add to Timeline at Playhead**

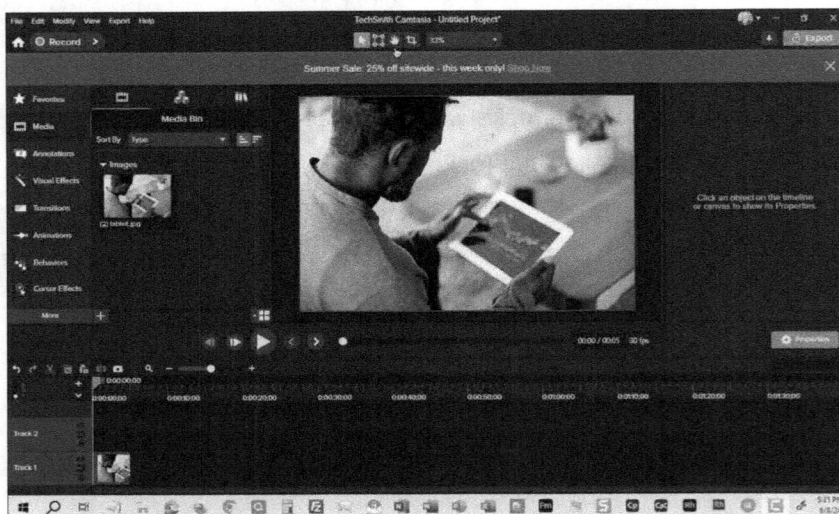

   ☐ choose **File > Import > Media**

   ☐ from **Camtasia 2025 Book Assets > Video Files**, open **CreateNewFolderVideo.trec**

   ☐ on the **Media Bin**, right-click the video and choose **Add to Timeline at Playhead**

3. Extend the playtime of an image.

   ☐ on the **Timeline**, stretch the tablet media in Track 1 until its playtime is equal to the playtime of the video in Track 2

4. Use the Corner Pin feature to fit the video within the tablet image.

   ☐ on the **Canvas**, resize the **video** media to approximately one-third of its current size, roughly the size of the tablet in the background image

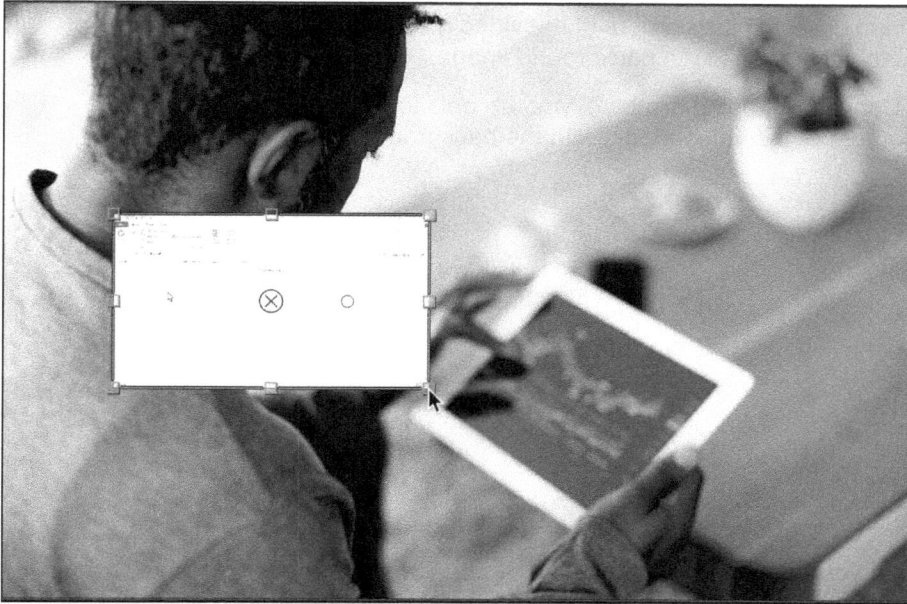

   ☐ with the video media selected, click the **Corner Pin Mode** icon ▦ (the icon is grouped with a few other tools just above the Canvas)

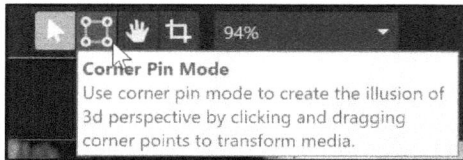

   ☐ on the **Canvas**, drag the video media over the image of the tablet in the background (if the video is a bit too large or too small, you can resize it later)

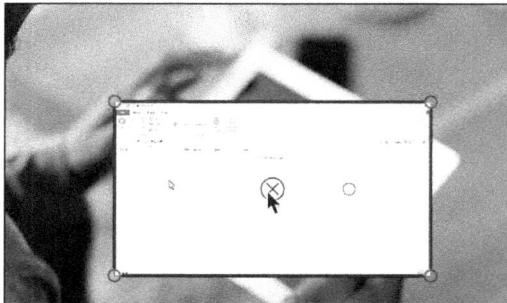

   ☐ on the **Canvas**, **drag** the **top left corner** of the video media until it matches the top left corner of the screen within the tablet image

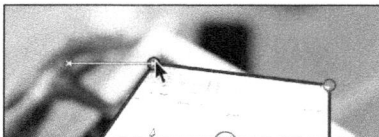

NOTES

NOTES

Corner Pin Mode Confidence Check

1. If necessary, choose **View > Enable Canvas Snapping** to **disable** the feature. (Remove the checkmark from beside the menu item.)

2. Continue dragging the corners of the video media to match the shape of the tablet screen in the background image.

   With Canvas Snapping disabled, you are able to more precisely match the corners of the video media with the background image.

   Note: If you need to resize the video, return to **Edit** mode. If you need to make more edits to the video skew, return to Corner Pin Mode.

   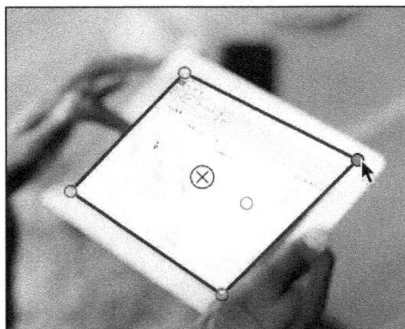

3. Preview the results.

   How cool is it be able to seamlessly integrate an image with a video?

4. Save the project to the **Camtasia 2025 Book Assets > Projects** folder as **MyCornerPinMode**.

iCONLOGiC™

Module 5: Audio

In This Module You Will Learn About:

- Audio Media, page 94
- Voice Narration, page 99
- Splitting Media, page 103
- Audio Editing, page 105

And You Will Learn To:

- Add Music From the Library, page 94
- Fade Audio, page 97
- Record Voice Narration, page 100
- Split Audio Media, page 103
- Rename Tracks, page 105
- Silence Audio, Ripple Delete, and Use AI Noise Removal, page 106

NOTES

Audio Media

You can import four audio media types into a Camtasia project: WAV, MP3, WMA, and M4A. The most common audio formats among the four types are WAV and MP3.

WAV (WAVE): WAV files are one of the original digital audio standards. Although high in quality, WAV files can be large. Typical WAV audio files can easily take up to several megabytes of storage per minute of playing time. If your learner has a slow Internet connection, the download time for large files is unacceptable. **MP3** (MPEG Audio Layer III): Developed in Germany by the Fraunhofer Institute, MP3 files are compressed digital audio files. File sizes in this format are typically 90 percent smaller than WAV files.

You will find a few sound files in the Camtasia Library, and there are additional resources among the TechSmith Camtasia audio assets at **https://library.techsmith.com/camtasia** via a paid subscription. According to TechSmith, you can use their media assets in a Camtasia project royalty-free. When something from a trusted source is labeled royalty-free, it means you can confidently use those assets without the need to pay additional fees to the copyright holder. However, before using assets obtained from any other source, you should ensure you have documented permission to use those assets for your intended purpose.

Guided Activity 31: Add Music From the Library

1. Using Camtasia, open and upgrade the **AudioMe** project from **Camtasia 2025 Book Assets > Projects**.

2. Add background music to the project from the Library.

   ❑ on the **Timeline**, ensure the **Playhead** is positioned at the **beginning**

   ❑ click the **Media** tool at the left and then click **Library** 📚

   ❑ from the **Library** drop-down menu, ensure that **Camtasia 2025** is selected

   ❑ on the **Library**, open the **Audio** folder

   ❑ right-click any of the audio files and choose **Add to Timeline at Playhead**

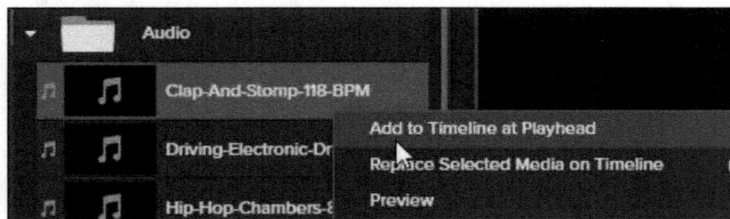

   The audio media appears on the Timeline in Track 2.

Library Audio Confidence Check

1. Use the Canvas to preview the project and hear the music.

2. On the **Timeline**, **select** and **delete** the audio media you just added.

3. On the **Media Bin**, notice that although you've removed the music from the Timeline, a copy of the unused media asset is retained in the Bin.

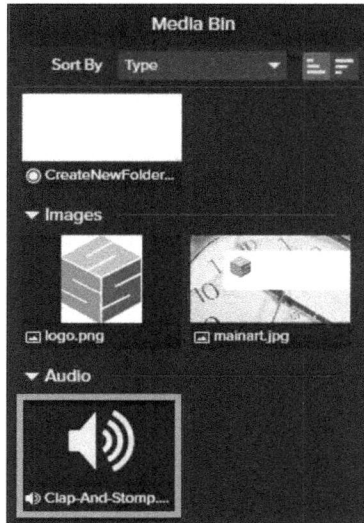

4. From the **Library**, add a different audio file to the Timeline.

5. Preview the project to hear the music.

6. on the **Timeline**, **select** and **delete** the music.

7. On the **Media Bin,** notice that the music is shown even though it is no longer being used on the Timeline (along with the first music track you added).

8. Right-click the Media Bin and choose **Delete Unused Media**.

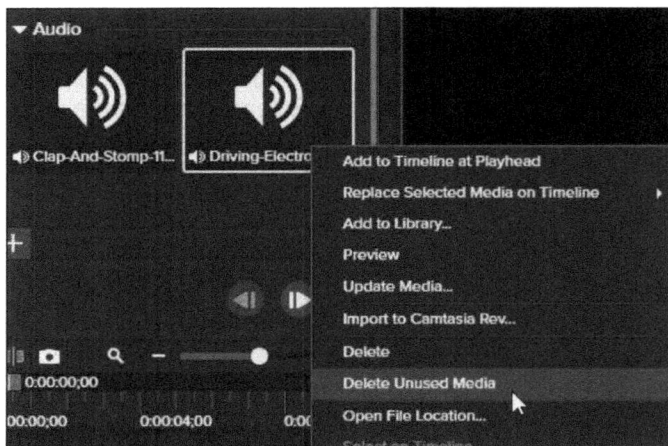

Note: Deleting unused media isn't a requirement but does keep the Media Bin clutter-free and will reduce the size of the overall project folder.

9. Save the project.

NOTES

Guided Activity 32: Import Background Music

1. Ensure that the **AudioMe** project is open.

2. Import an audio file to the Media Bin.

   ☐ choose **File > Import > Media**

   ☐ navigate to **Camtasia 2025 Book Assets > Audio Files**

   ☐ from the **Audio Files** folder, open/import **2Step1.mp3**

   The imported music track appears in the Media Bin.

3. Add the imported audio to the Timeline.

   ☐ ensure the **Playhead** is positioned at the **beginning** of the **Timeline**

   ☐ on the **Media Bin**, right-click **2Step1.mp3** and choose **Add to Timeline at Playhead**

   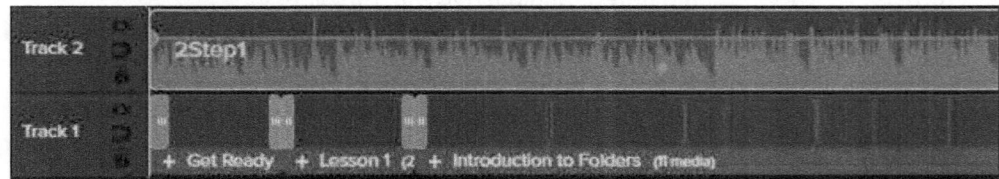

4. Preview the project to hear the music you just added to the Timeline.

   If you listen to the music until the end, you'll notice that the audio fades out nicely. However, if you preview the beginning of the project, you'll notice that the music starts just a bit too abruptly. You will take care of that next when you learn how to fade audio.

Guided Activity 33: Fade Audio

1. Ensure that the **AudioMe** project is open.

2. Fade audio in.

   ☐ on the **Timeline**, select the **2Step1** music track on **Track 2**

   ☐ from the tools at the left, click **Audio Effects**

   ☐ from the **Audio Effects** panel, right-click **Fade In** and choose **Add to Selected Media**

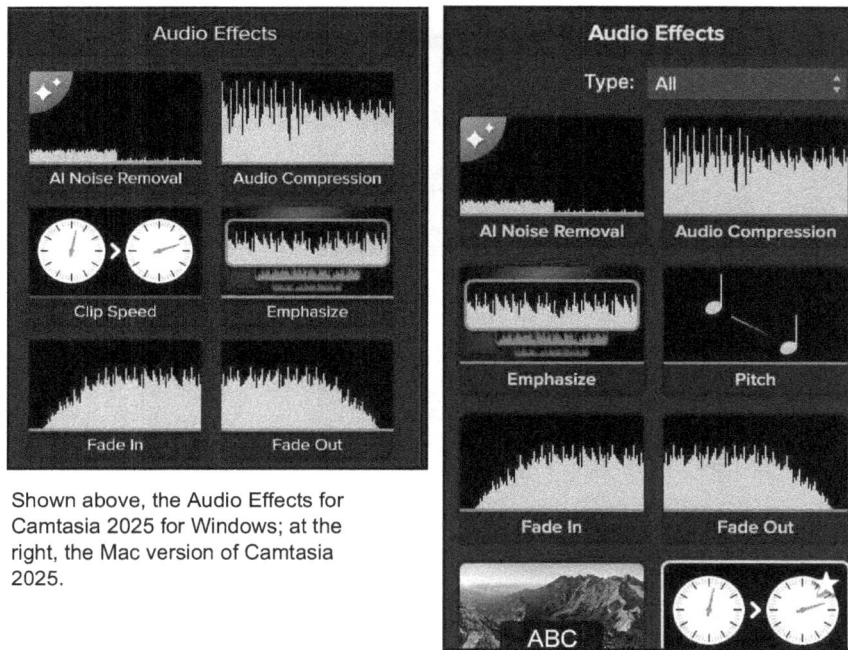

Shown above, the Audio Effects for Camtasia 2025 for Windows; at the right, the Mac version of Camtasia 2025.

Notice that a "ramp" has been added to the left side of the media.

The ramp begins at the bottom of the media and then gets taller until the audio hits a consistent level. You can manually drag the green line to control how the audio fades in, but you'll probably be happy with the level established automatically by Camtasia.

3. Preview the beginning of the project to hear the audio fade-in.

4. If you'd like the fade effect to last a bit longer, drag the green circle on the audio media **right** to extend the fade timing.

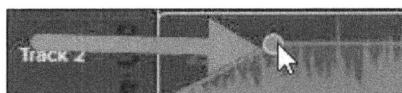

NOTES

NOTES

Fading Confidence Check

1. Delete the background music from the Timeline.

2. Using the Library, add any Music Track to the Timeline.

   The music that you just added to the Timeline likely plays far longer than your other Timeline assets.

3. Drag the **right side** of the background music **left** until the end of the music lines up with the assets in the last group on the **Timeline**.

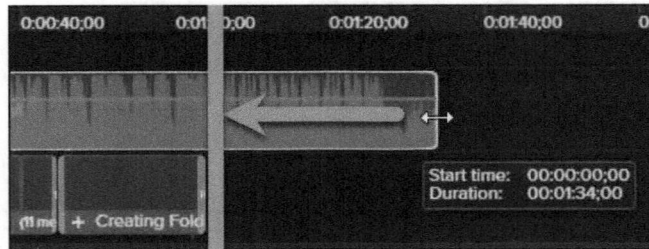

4. Use the **Audio Effects** to add **Fade In** and/or **Fade Out** effects to the music on the **Timeline** as you see fit.

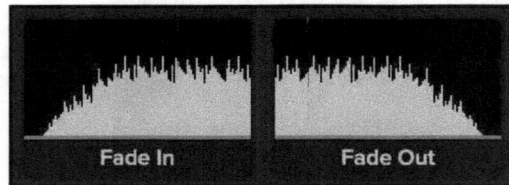

5. Preview the project to hear the fade effects.

6. Save the project. (Mac users: You can close the project.)

Voice Narration

Camtasia allows you to record your voice and sound effects and add them to the Timeline. If you plan to record audio, consider the following:

Voiceover Scripts: There is a script called **CreatingFoldersVoiceoverScript** in **Camtasia 2025 Book Assets > Other Assets**. You'll be opening that script soon. It's a good idea to write and then rehearse the voiceover script before recording the audio in Camtasia. Rehearsals are the perfect opportunity to find any areas of the script that will cause you problems while recording (trouble pronouncing words, for example, or wordiness).

Location, Location, Location: You might be surprised by how much noise there is in an average office or home. Is there a nearby faucet dripping? Is the overhead fan making noise? Is your neighbor or family member coughing or sneezing? You may be creating your eLearning at home, where you're sure it's quieter. But is the dog barking? Are the kids playing just outside your door? While you have become adept at tuning out everyday sounds, your microphone hears—and records—everything. Before using your office or cubicle as a recording studio, stop and listen to what's happening around you, and try to get your surroundings as quiet as possible.

Microphones vs. Headsets: A microphone is what you'll use to record your audio. It can be positioned on your desk, on a stand, suspended from the ceiling, or attached to your clothing. Typical headsets combine a microphone, typically a boom that can be adjusted up and down and further or closer to your mouth, and a listening device. As the name implies, a headset is usually positioned on your head. You can use either a microphone or a headset when you record audio. If you'd like to see and hear a side-by-side comparison of several recording devices, **Rick Zanotti** is an excellent resource. Visit **youtube.com** and search for "**eLearnChat Microphones for eLearning**" for an entire video series Rick created that covers everything from Sennheiser to Shure to Neumann to Blue Bird.

Microphone Placement: The microphone should be positioned approximately six inches from your mouth to reduce the chance that nearby sounds will be recorded. Ideally, you should position the microphone above your nose and pointed down at your mouth. Also, if you position the microphone just to the side of your mouth, you can soften the sound of the letters S and P.

Microphone Technique: It's a good idea to keep a glass of water close and, just before recording, take a drink. To eliminate breathing and lip-smack sounds, turn away from the microphone, take a deep breath, exhale, take another deep breath, open your mouth, turn back toward the microphone, and start speaking. Speak slowly. When recording for the first time, many people race through the content. *Take your time.*

Monitor Your Audio Level As You Record: When recording your audio, you will see an Input Level meter on Camtasia's Voice Narration panel indicating how well the recording process is going. When the meter is green to yellow, you're fine. However, when the meter is orange to red, you are being warned that you are too close to the microphone or speaking too loudly.

NOTES

NOTES

Guided Activity 34: Record Voice Narration

1. Using a word processor, open **CreatingFoldersVoiceoverScript** from **Camtasia 2025 Book Assets > Other_Assets**.

Let's pretend for a moment that you've been hired to serve as the voiceover talent for the eLearning project. It's quite possible you'd get a script similar to the file you've just opened.

Audio File 1:
Welcome to Super Simplistic Solutions learning series.
This is lesson one: Creating New Folders.

Audio File 2:
This lesson is going to teach you how to create a new folder on your computer, how to rename it, and how to both delete and restore recycled items.

Audio File 3:
When creating folders keep in mind that you can create as many folders as you need.

---

2. Rehearse the audio script.

   ❒ using a measured (not too fast nor too slow) cadence, read the following out loud:

   Welcome to Super Simplistic Solutions learning series.

   This is lesson one: Creating New Folders.

   Next you'll record your voice in Camtasia. You can close the script now if you'd like.

3. Using Camtasia, open **NarrateMe** from the **Camtasia 2025 Book Assets > Projects** folder.

4. Record voiceover audio.

   ❒ on the **Timeline**, position the Playhead on the **Lesson 1** group

   ❒ from the tools at the left, click **Voice Narration**

On the **Voice Narration** panel, notice that I have already added the part of the voiceover script you'll be recording. Alternatively, you could print the script document and have it beside you during the recording phase.

☐ if necessary, select **your microphone** from the drop-down menu at the top of the Voice Narration panel

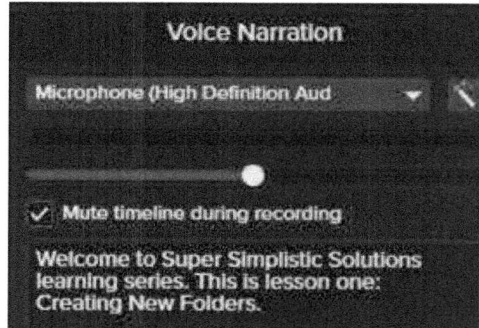

☐ ensure **Mute timeline during recording** is selected

Muting the Timeline during recording is a good idea for this video because you have background audio on Track 2. If you don't mute the audio, the music could play through your computer speakers and ruin your voiceover audio.

And now, prepare yourself! Once you start the recording process, there isn't a count-down or any kind of warning. Instead, Camtasia simply starts recording. While you are recording, the video will play on the Canvas so you can see what's happening in your project while you narrate.

☐ click the **Start Voice Recording** button

There's a slight difference between the Mac and PC when it comes to recording audio. In the image above at the left, the Start Voice Recording button for PC users does not have a microphone icon. When finished recording audio on the PC, you are prompted to give the audio file a name. On the Mac, recorded audio is automatically saved and the media added to the Timeline.

☐ using a slow, deliberate cadence, read the following out loud:

Welcome to Super Simplistic Solutions learning series.

This is lesson one: Creating New Folders.

5. When finished, click the **Stop** button.

PC users, the Save Narration As dialog box opens.
Mac users, the audio is automatically saved and added to the Timeline.

6. PC users only: Name the file **My_Lesson1_Voiceover** and save it to the **Audio Files** folder within the **Camtasia 2025 Book Assets** folder.

NOTES

All users, your voiceover narration appears on a new track on the Timeline. In addition, the new audio has been added to the Media Bin.

7. Preview the project.

   You should be able to hear your new voiceover audio. However, notice that the audio is hard to hear because the background music is playing at the same time. You'll fix that shortly.

8. Save the project. (Mac users: You can close the project.)

Splitting Media

You will find Camtasia's ability to split media segments on the Timeline to be a valuable feature. Have you imported an audio clip that's too long and difficult to manage? Click at the top of Timeline where you want to split the audio clip and quickly split the clip into as many segments as you need. Want to add a transition in the middle of a video clip? Because transitions cannot be inserted in the middle of a clip, click where you need a transition and insert a split.

Guided Activity 35: Split Audio Media

1. Using Camtasia, open **SplitMe** from the **Camtasia 2025 Book Assets > Projects** folder.

   This is basically the same project you were just working on except the voiceover audio that you recorded and inserted during the last activity has been replaced by a file named **audio_file01**.

2. Preview the project and notice, as mentioned at the end of the last activity, the background music and voiceover audio are playing at the same time, making it difficult to understand what the narrator is saying.

3. Lock Tracks.

   ❏ at the far left of the Timeline, click the padlock icon to the left of **Track 1** and **Track 3** to **lock** those tracks (only **Track 2** should remain unlocked)

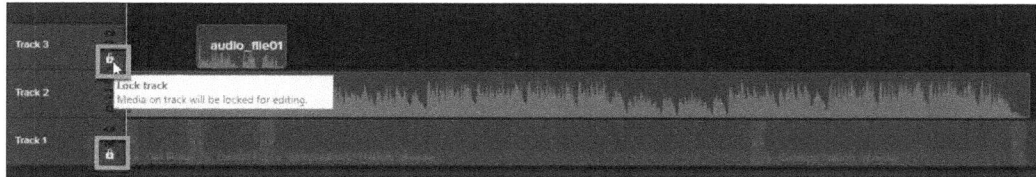

   You are about to split the background music into two parts and then manipulate the two audio pieces on the Timeline so they don't conflict with the voiceover audio. During the splitting process, it's possible not only to split the background music but also to split media in other tracks inadvertently. Now that you have locked two of the three tracks, only the unlocked media in Track 2 will be affected.

4. Split the background music in Track 2 into two segments.

   ❏ on the **Timeline**, position the Playhead at the **4;29** mark

   ❏ on the **Timeline**, select the media in **Track 2**

   ❏ right-click the **Playhead** and choose **Split Selected**

   The music track is split into two parts (as shown in the second image above).

TechSmith Camtasia: The Essentials (2025 Edition)

NOTES

Audio Timing Confidence Check

1. Select the second (larger) segment of the background music.

2. Drag the **left edge** of the segment to the **right** until it lines up with the end of the **audio_file01** media in **Track 3**.

3. On Track 2, select the **first segment of the background music** and, using the **Audio Effects** panel, **Fade Out** the media.

4. On Track 2, select the **second segment of the background music** and **Fade In** the media.

5. Preview the project.

   The background music stops when the narrator begins to speak. Nice. The music does not start again until *after* the narrator is finished speaking.

   There's a problem now with the timing for Lesson 1 group. The group isn't on the Canvas quite long enough to match the voiceover audio. To fix that, you'll need to change the timing of a few Timeline objects.

6. Save the project. (Mac users: You can close the project.)

Audio Editing

Earlier in this module, you learned how to edit an audio clip by fading the volume in and out. Camtasia offers you other editing options, such as the ability to cut segments of a waveform and even to replace unwanted audio with silence.

During this module you will also get a chance to use the **AI Noise Removal** tool, a powerful audio effect that automatically detects and removes unwanted background noise from your recordings using artificial intelligence. It's especially useful for cleaning up audio that includes persistent hums, static, or environmental sounds like fans, air conditioners, or distant chatter—without affecting the clarity of your voice.

Guided Activity 36: Rename Tracks

1. Open and upgrade/convert the **EditMyAudio** project.

   This project is similar to the project you were just working on with a few notable exceptions. First, all of the tracks are unlocked. Second, two of the tracks, Voiceover and Background Audio, have names that are more descriptive than the default names Track 1, Track 2, etc. There's also additional voiceover audio in the Voiceover track.

2. Rename a track.

   ☐ on the far left of the Timeline, double-click the name **Track 1**

   ☐ replace the text with the word **Main** and press [**enter**]

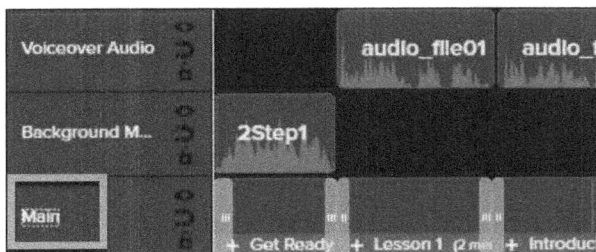

   While naming Timeline tracks is optional, I find it's a helpful step especially when dealing with larger projects that contain more than a few tracks.

NOTES

Guided Activity 37: Silence Audio, Ripple Delete, and Use AI Noise Removal

1. Ensure that the **EditMyAudio** project is open.

2. Preview an audio clip.

   ☐ on the **Media Bin**, double-click **audio_file02_silence** to preview the media

   There are two strange sounds in the clip, and there's a bit of dead air at the end of the audio file. You have two choices for removing unwanted audio segments: delete the content or replace the content with **Silence**. When you delete the content, the media's duration is reduced by the amount of audio that is deleted. However, if your goal is to remove a problem in the audio clip (such as click sounds) without altering the duration of the media, using Silence is an ideal solution.

3. Close the media's **Preview** window.

4. Lock both the **Background** and **Main** tracks.

   As you learned earlier, locking a track ensures changes made to other unlocked tracks will not affect locked tracks.

5. Replace a selection of audio with silence.

   ☐ on the **Voiceover Audio** track, double-click **audio_file02_silence** to position the Playhead at the beginning of the audio file

   ☐ at the top of the **Timeline**, drag the **Zoom** slider **right** to zoom much closer to the Timeline

   At this enhanced view, you can get a better look at the waveform that makes up the audio file. You can see that the narrator's audio levels are consistent across the wave.

Take a look at about the **15 second** mark on the Timeline. There's a spike in the wave that isn't consistent with the rest of the wave. This part of the wave is an erroneous sound that you need to remove.

☐ position the **Playhead** to the beginning of the errant sound

☐ on the **Playhead**, drag the red box **right** to highlight the sound

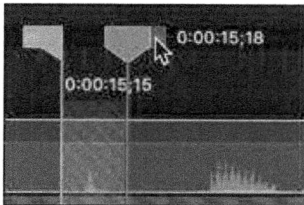

☐ on the **Timeline**, right-click the selection and choose **Silence Audio**

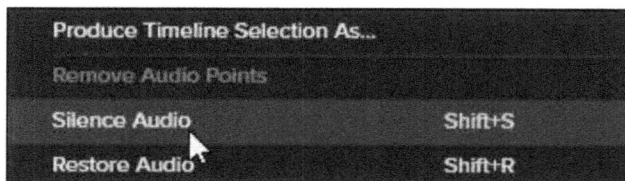

The errant sound is removed without altering the playtime of the media.

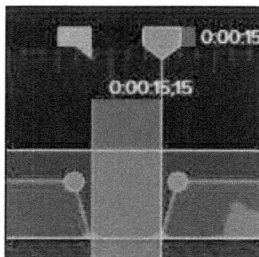

6. On the Timeline, double-click the Playhead.

The green and red selection boxes on the Playhead snap back to the Playhead.

NOTES

NOTES

7. Delete selected media.

❑ on the **Timeline**, scroll **right** to the end of the **audio_file02_silence** media

There is **dead air** in the audio_file02_silence media that you can delete.

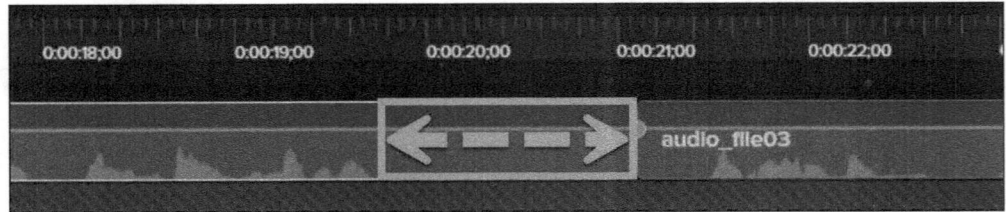

❑ on the **Timeline**, position the Playhead at **19;21** (this is the point in the media where the narrator is finished speaking and then there's dead air)

❑ drag the Playhead's red box to the **right** to highlight through the end of the **audio_file02_silence** media

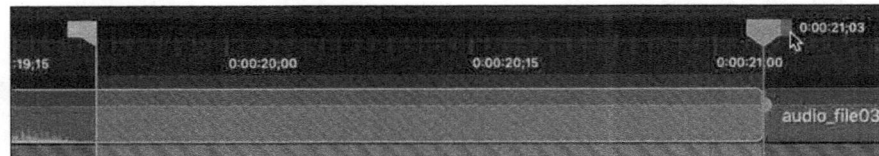

❑ right-click the selection and choose **Delete** (PC) or **Delete Range** (Mac)

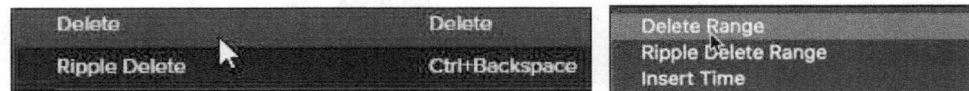

The selected portion of the audio clip is removed but you've now got **a sizable gap** on the Timeline. Instead of simply deleting a selection, you can delete both the content and the gap by using **Ripple Delete** instead of Delete.

8. Undo the last step.

❑ choose **Edit > Undo**

9. Ripple Delete selected media.

❑ ensure that the dead air is still selected in the **Voiceover** track

❑ PC users, right-click the selection and choose **Ripple Delete**
Mac users, right-click the selection and choose **Ripple Delete Range**

On the Timeline, the gap to the right of the deleted content is filled automatically by track content to the right of the selection.

Audio Editing Confidence Check

There's another errant sound at about the 16-second mark on the **Timeline**.

1. Select and then replace the sound with Silence.

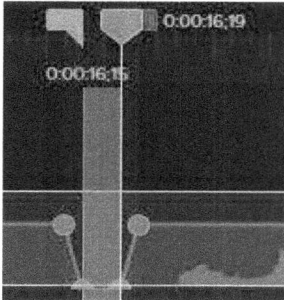

    Note: Remember to double-click the Playhead to return it to its default setting (the green and red boxes will snap back to the Playhead).

2. Save the project. (Mac users: You can close the project.)

3. Create a new project.

4. From the **Library**, open **Audio Visualizers**.

5. Add **Audio Wave** to the Timeline at the **Playhead**.

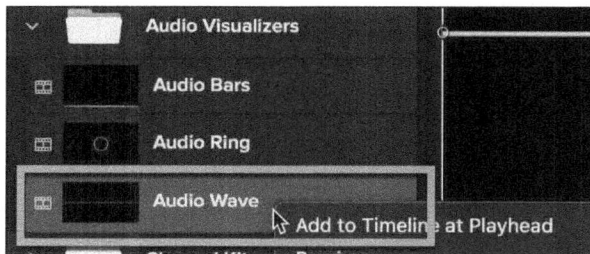

6. Preview the media using the **Play** button on the Canvas.

    Underwhelmed? Sure. The Audio Wave isn't doing anything at the moment. As a matter of fact, it will remain "flat-lined" until you pair it with media containing audio.

7. Return the **Playhead** to the **far left** of the Timeline.

8. From the **Library**, open **Audio**.

9. Add **any of the audio files** to the Timeline at the **Playhead**.

10. Preview the media using the **Play** button on the Canvas.

    Now that's more like it. The Audio Wave media has built-on behaviors that allow it to dance to the beat of the music. Pretty cool stuff, yes?

    You'll find all kinds of fun "toys" in the Library. Spend some time adding them and thinking about how the provided media can enhance your training videos.

11. Delete all of the Timeline media.

12. Delete all unused media from the Media Bin.

13. Import the following audio into the Media Bin: **Remove my noise with AI.wav**.

NOTES

NOTES

14. Add the **Remove my noise with AI** audio file to the Timeline.

15. Preview the audio.

    There is an unnecessary amount of "dead air" at the beginning of the audio, and more concerning, static is present throughout the entire recording. (You may need to increase the volume on your headset or computer speakers to hear it.)

    While replacing portions audio media with silence has worked in the past, you can't rely on the Silence Audio feature this time because the static is consistent throughout the media. And although you could spend time identifying speech gaps and silencing them, you won't be able to remove the static from the parts of the waveform that contain audio you want to keep.

    This is the perfect scenario for using the **AI Noise Removal** tool.

16. On the **Timeline**, select the audio media.

17. On the **Audio Effects** group of tools, right-click **AI Noise Removal** and choose **Add to Selected Media**.

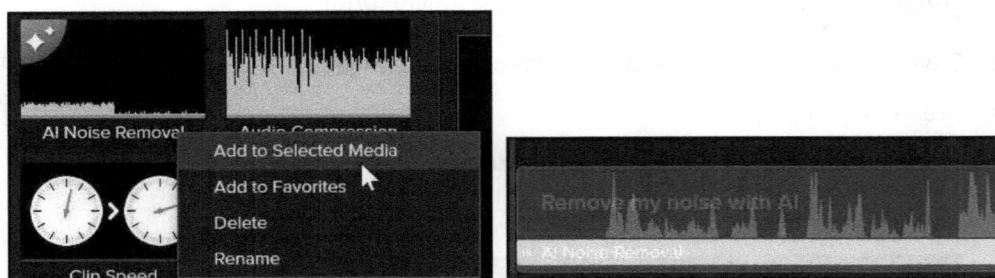

18. Preview the audio.

    Like magic, the static is removed from the Timeline media. The default setting for AI Noise Removal is 80. You can increase the noise removal level up to 100 in the Effects area of the Properties panel. In my experience, 80 works well, but if you still hear background static, try experimenting with a higher value.

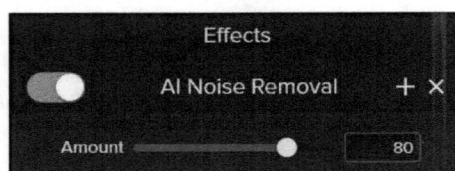

19. Edit the audio to remove any unnecessary gaps, background noise, or verbal flubs as appropriate.

20. Save the project as **My AI Audio Edits**.

21. Mac users, you can close the project.
    PC users, the project will close automatically when you open the next project.

---

iCONLOGiC™

Module 6: Exporting

In This Module You Will Learn About:

- Video and Web Output, page 112
- Camtasia Rev, page 120

And You Will Learn To:

- Export a Project as a Video, page 112
- Export a Project as a Website, page 115
- Export and Upload to YouTube, page 117
- Record Screen Actions with Rev, page 120

NOTES

Video and Web Output

As you have worked through the first several modules in this book, you learned how to record a video using the Recorder (page 28). Beginning on page 44, you learned how to add videos to the Editor. You added images (page 50), annotations/captions (page 72), behaviors/animations (page 82), and audio (page 93).

To create or edit eLearning with Camtasia, you need a licensed copy of Camtasia. When your project is finished, you need to export the project as a video or as a website. In addition to being able to export to your local computer and manually uploading the output to a serve, there are export options allowing you to export directly to media servers like Screencast and YouTube. In short, you need Camtasia to create and edit Camtasia projects. Your learners do not. Once you export your Camtasia project, learners can view your content on devices such as desktop computers, laptops, and mobile devices (smartphones, tablets, etc.).

Guided Activity 38: Export a Project as a Video

1. Using Camtasia, open and upgrade the **ExportMe** project.

2. Export the project as a video.

   ❑ choose **Export > Local File**

   The Export As dialog box opens.

   ❑ change the **Export As** name to **Create New Folders**
   ❑ browse to and open **Camtasia 2025 Book Assets > Produced Videos**

Export As:	Create New Folders
Tags:	

   📁 Produced Videos

   ❑ from the **File format** (Mac) or **File type** (PC) drop-down menu, ensure that **Export to MP4** (Mac) or **MP4** (PC) is selected

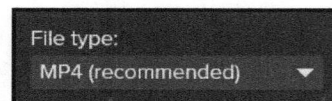

   File format: Export to MP4 (.mp4)   Options...

   File type:
   MP4 (recommended)

   ❑ click the **Export** button

The project exports. You can track the export progress via the dialog box shown below. The Mac dialog box is shown first; the PC version is shown in the second image. While your project is exporting, you won't be able to work within Camtasia without first canceling the export process.

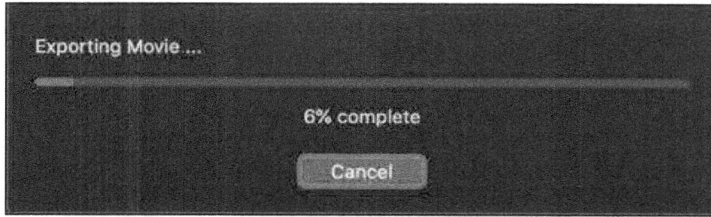

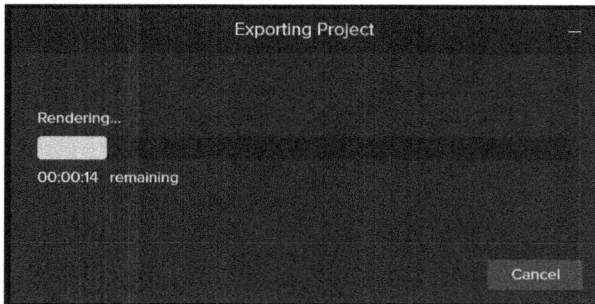

Exporting Movie ...

6% complete

Cancel

Exporting Project —

Rendering...

00:00:14 remaining

Cancel

Once the export process is complete, you'll see one of the dialog boxes below (Mac is on the left; PC is on the right).

Export finished

Close

Reveal in Finder

☐ Don't show again

Exporter

✓ Your media successfully exported.

Close   View Media   Open File Location

❏ Mac users, click the **Reveal in Finder** button; PC users, click **Open File Location**

The Produced Videos folder opens. The only file in the folder at this point is the single video that you just exported.

Name	^	Date Modified	Size	Kind
Create N...ders.mp4		Today at 1:28 PM	23.2 MB	MPEG-4 movie

Name	Date	Type	Size	Length
Create New Folders....	4/17/25 1:44 PM	MP4 File	6,152 KB	00:01:08

NOTES

NOTES

3. Open the video file in a media player.

❑ double-click the video to open it in your default media player

❑ click the **Play** button on the playbar to start the video

Believe it or not, you are now a published eLearning author. Congratulations!

4. Close the media player.

5. Return to the Camtasia project.

Guided Activity 39: Export a Project as a Website

1. Ensure that the **ExportMe** project is open.

2. Export the project as a Web Page.

   ☐ choose **Export > Local File**

   ☐ change the **Export As** name to **Create New Folders**

   ☐ browse to and open **Camtasia 2025 Book Assets > Produced Videos**

   ☐ Mac users, from the **File format** drop-down menu, ensure that **Export to MP4**; from beneath the **Caption Style** area, select **Export as Web Page**

   File format: Export to MP4 (.mp4) ⇕ Options...

   ☑ Export as Web Page

   ☐ PC users, from the **File Type** drop-down menu choose **MP4 with Smart Player**

   File name: Create New Folders | File type: MP4 with Smart Player ▾

   ☐ All users, click the **Export** button

3. Review the website contents.

   ☐ once the export process is complete, click **Reveal in Finder** (Mac) or **Open File Location** (PC).

   The last time you exported the project, you exported as a video which yielded a single file. This time, you've created a website with the folder with assets that rely on each other to correctly work in a browser. When you upload these assets to a web server, the assets must be kept together.

   The output is a bit different between the Mac and the PC. On the Mac, there's a single html file in the folder: **index.html**. This is the start page for the lesson. There is also a media folder containing several required assets. On the PC, the start page is called **Create New Folders**.html and there's a scripts folder.

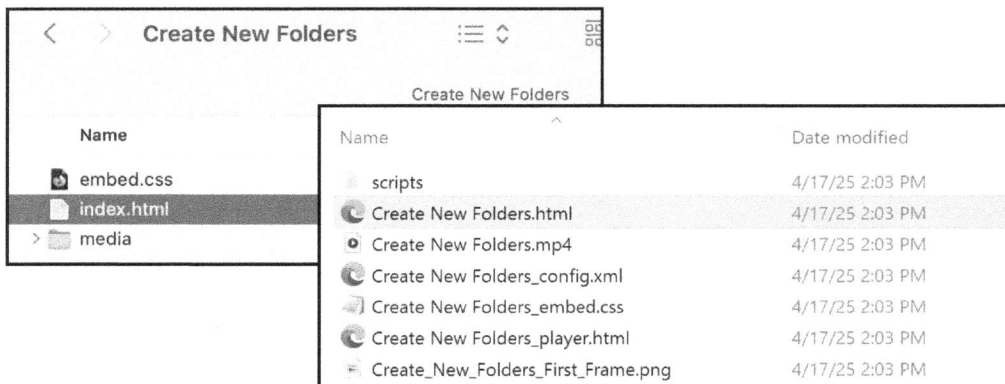

< > Create New Folders	≔ ◇	🔠

   Create New Folders

Name		Name	Date modified
🅰 embed.css		scripts	4/17/25 2:03 PM
📄 index.html		Ⓒ Create New Folders.html	4/17/25 2:03 PM
> 📁 media		⊙ Create New Folders.mp4	4/17/25 2:03 PM
		Ⓒ Create New Folders_config.xml	4/17/25 2:03 PM
		Create New Folders_embed.css	4/17/25 2:03 PM
		Ⓒ Create New Folders_player.html	4/17/25 2:03 PM
		Create_New_Folders_First_Frame.png	4/17/25 2:03 PM

   NOTES

NOTES

4. View the exported web content in a web browser.

☐ Mac users, double-click **index.html**
   PC users, double-click **Create New Folders**.html

The web output opens in your default web browser.

☐ click the **Play** button in the middle of the screen to play the lesson

The output includes a "smart player" the appears if you point your mouse to the middle of the screen. The player automatically disappears after a few seconds.

5. Close the browser window.

6. Return to the Camtasia project.

Guided Activity 40: Export and Upload to YouTube

1. Ensure that the **ExportMe** project is open.

   Before you can export a video to YouTube, you need a YouTube account. If you do not already have a YouTube or Gmail account, go to **www.youtube.com** and set one up. Creating an account is free and usually on takes only a few moments.

2. Export a video directly to YouTube.

   ☐ choose **Export > YouTube**

   You'll be prompted to Sign in to your YouTube account.

   ☐ click the **Sign In** button and then follow the onscreen prompts to access your YouTube account

3. Give the video a Title, Description, and Tags (keywords).

   ☐ in the **Title** field, type **Creating New Folders**

   ☐ in the **Description** field, type **This demonstration will teach you how to create a folder using Windows.**

   ☐ in the **Tags** field, type **training, windows, file management**

   The tags make it easier for YouTube users to search YouTube and find your video.

   ☐ change the Category to **Education**

   ☐ leave the **Privacy** option set to **Public (anyone can search and view)**

NOTES

4. Export the video.

☐ click the **Export** button

The video is exported and automatically posted to your YouTube account.

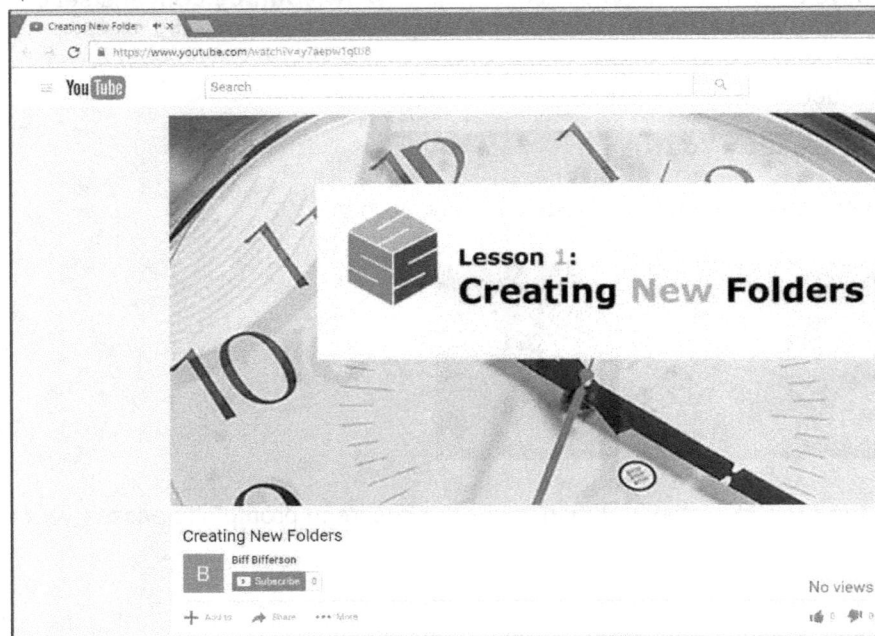

5. Close the web browser and return to Camtasia.

Sharing Projects Confidence Check

If you work with other Camtasia developers, you might be asked to share your project with team members so they can edit it. Sharing projects among Camtasia developers is not the same as using the Export menu to create output for a learner as you've learned to do during this module.

To share Camtasia production files with other Camtasia developers, follow these steps:

> **Mac to Windows:** To share a Mac-based project with someone who is using Camtasia 2025 for the PC, choose **File > Export > Project for Windows**.

> **Windows to Mac:** To share a PC-based project with someone who is using Camtasia 2025 for the Mac, choose **File > Export > Project for Mac**.

> **Share Projects Mac to Mac:** Sharing a project with other Mac developers is simple. When saving the project, ensure that you select **Create standalone project**. Send a team member the project file (the **cmproj** file), and you're set. The **cmproj** file is a self-contained collection of all project assets. If team members have the same or newer version of Camtasia as you, can open and edit the project.

> **Share Projects PC to PC:** When saving the project, select **Create standalone project**. Send the project folder to the other Camtasia developer. The project folder will likely contain several assets so zipping the project is recommended. Those steps follow.

> **Note:** The steps below are for PC users only. Mac users, save and close all projects and then skip ahead to the Camtasia Rev section beginning on page 120.

1. PC users, choose **File > Export > Zipped Project**.

2. Browse to a save destination of your choice.

3. Click the **Save** button.

   The resulting zip file contains the Camtasia project and all of the project's assets. Assuming the recipient of the zip file has the same version of Camtasia as you, team member can extract the contents, open, the tscproj file and then edit, and export the project as needed.

   ```
   ExportMe.zip

      Files/Folders in Zip file: 9
      2Step1.mp3
      audio_file01.wav
      audio_file02.wav
      audio_file03.wav
      audio_file04.wav
      CreateNewFolderVideo.trec
      ExportMe.tscproj
      logo.png
      mainart.jpg
   ```

4. Save the project.

NOTES

NOTES

Camtasia Rev

You learned to use Artificial Intelligence (AI) to remove static from an audio file (see page 110). Camtasia Rev introduces AI to your recording and production workflow.

If you enable Camtasia Rev on the Camtasia Recorder and then record your screen actions as you learned beginning on page 25, a screen appears when you stop recording that allows you to format your recording with dimensions optimized for specific sharing platforms. Using Rev, you can select a design layout and step through additional formatting options, such as choosing a background color, effects, and filters. Each Rev formatting choice is immediately shown onscreen, meaning your production level of effort goes down dramatically. Once you finish working through Rev, you can export the file locally, or publish directly to YouTube or Screencast.

Guided Activity 41: Record Screen Actions with Rev

1. All users, start Notepad (PC) or TextEdit (Mac) and, if necessary, rehearse the process of once again changing the page orientation.

   You learned about Notepad, TextEdit, and rehearsals beginning on page 26.

2. Back in Camtasia, create a **new project**.

3. From the top left of the Camtasia window, click the **Record** button.

4. Select the Notepad or TextEdit application as the recording region.

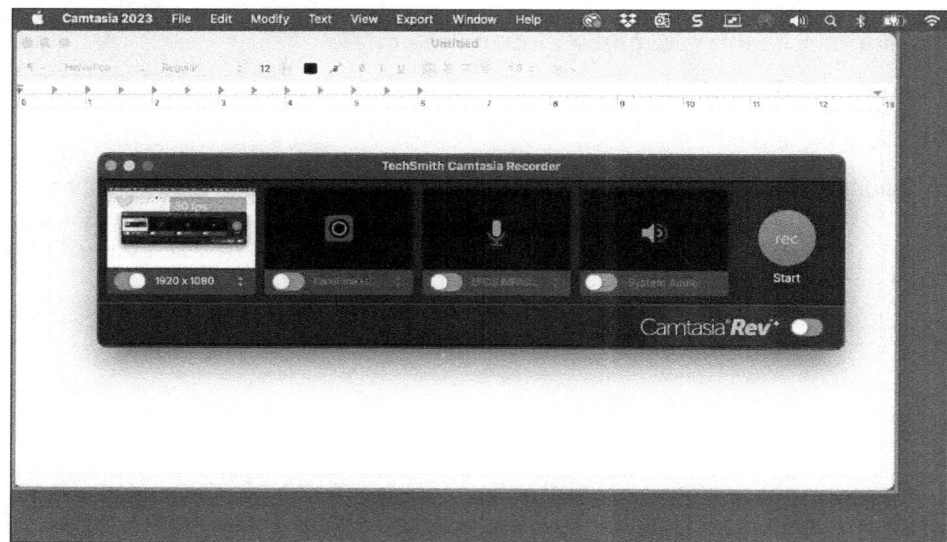

5. Enable Rev.

   ❏ from the bottom right of the Camtasia Recorder, click the Camtasia Rev **toggle**

   Camtasia Rev is enabled if the toggle is **green**.

Rev Confidence Check

1. Review the recording process that you learned beginning on page 28.

2. With Rev enabled, record the process of changing the page orientation of TextEdit or Notepad just like you did earlier.

3. When finished, stop the recording process.

4. Instead of sending your recording to Camtasia, the Camtasia Rev editor opens.

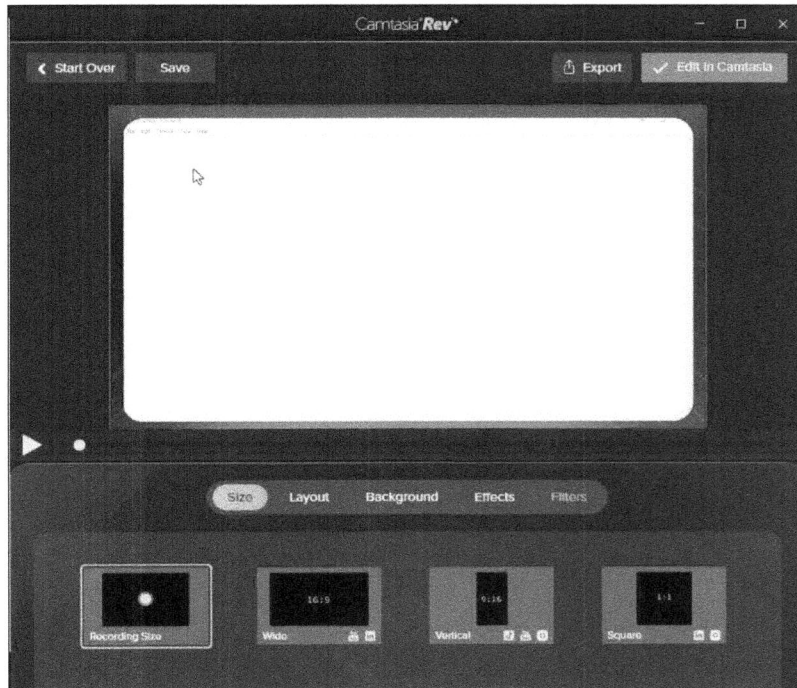

5. Notice that there are tabs in the middle of the Camtasia Rev window, including Size, Layout, and Background.

6. Notice that you can click **Start Over** to go back to the Camtasia recorder and re-record the video.

7. Notice that you can click **Edit in Camtasia** to open the Camtasia application and edit as you have learned during the activities in this book.

8. Click the **Size** tab and select any size that you like.

9. On the **Layout** tab, click through each of the layouts and select any one of them.

10. On the **Background** tab, click through each of the backgrounds and select any one of them.

11. On the **Effects** tab, select as many effects as you like.

    Because Rev is intended to lower your level of development effort, many Camtasia editing features are not available in Rev. You can combine Rev effects such as Border, Cursor Color, Highlight, and Cursor Scale. As mentioned above, you can **Edit in Camtasia** and change the effects, such as the cursor color. However, Rev does not have the editing power of Camtasia. Most editing tasks, such as controlling the Timeline, can only be accomplished in Camtasia.

NOTES

12. **Export** the recording as an **MP4** and name it **My first Rev video**.

13. When the export process is complete, view the media if you'd like.

14. When finished, close the video.

15. Close Camtasia Rev. (When asked if you'd like to save the Rev project, you can do so or delete it.)

16. On the Camtasia recorder, **disable** Camtasia Rev.

17. Close the Camtasia Recorder.

18. Back in Camtasia, click the Home icon. 🏠

19. On the **Home** tab, click **Open File in Camtasia Rev**.

20. Open **DeleteFolder.trec** from the **Camtasia 2025 Book Assets > Video Files** folder.

    The Camtasia Rev window reopens.

21. Click the **Size** tab and select any size that you like.

22. On the **Layout** tab, click through each of the layouts and select any one of them.

23. On the **Background** tab, click through each of the backgrounds and select any one of them.

24. On the **Effects** tab, select as many effects as you like.

25. Export the video as an **MP4** and give it the name **My second rev video**.

26. When the export process is complete, view the media if you'd like.

27. When finished, close the media.

28. Close Camtasia Rev. (When asked if you'd like to save the Rev project, you can do so or delete it.)

iCONLOGiC™

Module 7: Extending, Zooming, and Hotspots

In This Module You Will Learn About:

- Extending, page 124
- Zoom Animations, page 126
- Markers, page 130
- Hotspots, page 133

And You Will Learn To:

- Extend a Video Frame, page 124
- Add a Zoom-n-Pan Animation on the PC, page 126
- Add a Zoom Animation on the Mac, page 128
- Add a Timeline Marker, page 130
- Add an Interactive Hotspot, page 133

NOTES

Extending

If you record a software demonstration and then later record audio—as you learned to do on page 100—synchronizing the video with the audio can be challenging. During the following activity, you'll learn how to freeze a video on a single frame, making voiceover synchronization easier.

Guided Activity 42: Extend a Video Frame

1. Open and upgrade/convert the **ExtendZoomMe** project.

2. On the **Timeline**, notice that there is media in the Voiceover Audio track named **audio_file07** positioned on the Timeline at the **2:26;00 second mark**. (If necessary, zoom closer to the Timeline and scroll up to clearly see the media.)

3. Beginning at **2:26;00** on the **Timeline**, preview the project.

   In the video, the narrator is talking about the Recycle Bin and how its appearance has changed to indicate there's trash to be emptied. The video is just a bit ahead of the voiceover audio—in the video the mouse is circling around the Recycle Bin before the narrator mentions its appearance. Rather than re-record the video, you're going to freeze the video just long enough to synchronize the voiceover audio with the video.

4. Lock the Voiceover and Background Music tracks.

   ☐ at the **left** of the **Timeline**, click the **padlock** icon for both the **Voiceover** and **Background Music** tracks

   As you first learned on page 103, locking tracks prevents accidental changes. The media you are about to modify is on the **Main** track and you do not want to alter the other tracks.

5. Split a video into two segments.

   ☐ on the **Timeline**, click the **Zoom timeline in** icon to zoom closer to the Timeline media

❏ on the **Timeline**, drag the **Playhead** to **2:26;16** (if you cannot position the Playhead at exactly 2:26;16, trying zooming even closer to the Timeline)

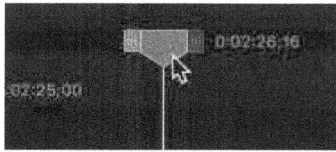

This is the point in the video just prior to the cursor moving toward the Recycle Bin.

❏ on the **Timeline**, **Main** track, select the **RestoreFolder** media

❏ right-click the **Playhead** and choose **Split Selected**

The video splits into two segments. One of the segments is significantly larger than the other.

6. Reposition a video segment.

❏ on the **Timeline**, position the **Playhead** at **2:29;05**

❏ on the **Timeline**, drag the **larger** of the two video segments **right** until it snaps to the Playhead's position at **2:29;05**

The gap between the two video segments is going to be filled by extending the last frame in the smaller segment.

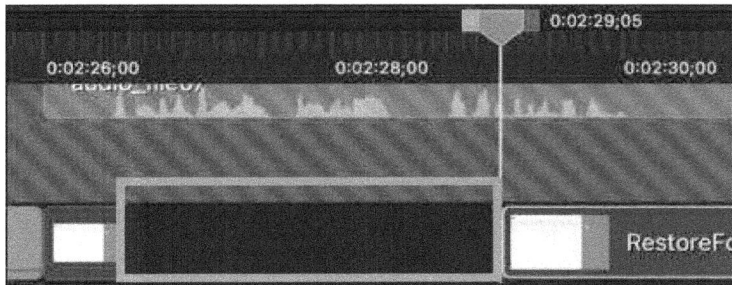

❏ double-click the **smaller video segment** to both select the media on the Timeline *and* move the Playhead in front of the media segment

❏ on your keyboard, press [**alt**] (PC) or [**option**] (Mac) and **drag** the **right edge** of the smaller video media right until it snaps to the larger segment

7. Preview from the beginning of the first RestoreFolder media.

Extending the frame has made the video freeze just long enough to allow the screen actions and voiceover audio to synchronize.

NOTES

NOTES

Zoom Animations

The Zoom-n-Pan feature is useful when the width and height of your project are large and you want to focus the learner's attention on a specific area of the screen. Zooming moves the learner closer to the screen, while Panning automatically moves the screen for the learner. Adding Zooms and Pans is as simple as positioning the Playhead where you want to add the effect, accessing the Zoom-n-Pan panel (via Animations), and stretching and/or moving the Zoom-n-Pan window.

> **Note:** The next activity is for PC users only. Mac users, your steps can be found on page 128.

Guided Activity 43: Add a Zoom-n-Pan Animation on the PC

1. Ensure that the **ExtendZoomMe** project is open.

2. Add a Zoom-n-Pan mark.

   ☐ on the **Timeline**, unlock the locked tracks (you locked the Background Music and Voiceover Audio tracks earlier)

   ☐ on the **Timeline**, position the Playhead at **0:47;27**

   On the Canvas, this is when the cursor has arrived at the Home tab and is about to click.

   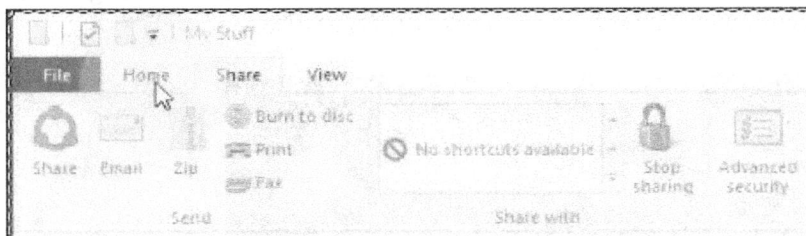

   ☐ from the list of tools at the left, click **Animations**

   There are two tabs: **Zoom-n-Pan** and **Animations**.

   ☐ select the **Zoom-n-Pan** tab

   ☐ on the **Zoom-n-Pan** panel, drag the lower right resizing handle **up** and to the **left** similar to the picture below

   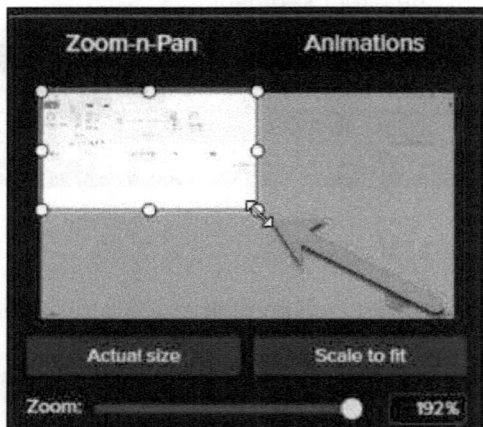

When you drag the resizing handle on the Zoom-n-Pan panel, the Canvas displays how close you've actually gotten to the screen.

On the Timeline, notice that the animation is represented by an arrow with two circles (one circle is at the arrowhead; the other circle is positioned at the left of the arrow). The circle on the left represents the beginning of the animation. The circle at the right represents the end of the animation. You can change the zoom percentage by selecting the tail or the head and changing the Scale on the Properties panel.

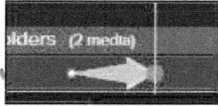

3. On the **Timeline**, position the **Playhead** a few seconds to the left of the zoom effect you just added.

4. Preview the project.

   Thanks to the Zoom-n-Pan, you are automatically zoomed closer to the action in the video.

5. Save the project.

   The next activity is for Mac users only. PC users, skip ahead to the "Add a Timeline Marker" activity that begins on page 130.

NOTES

NOTES

Guided Activity 44: Add a Zoom Animation on the Mac

1. Ensure that the **ExtendZoomMe** project is open.

2. Add a Zoom-n-Pan mark.

   ☐ on the **Timeline**, unlock any locked tracks

   ☐ position the Playhead at **47;27**

   This is the area of the video where the mouse pointer has arrived at the Home tab and is about to click.

   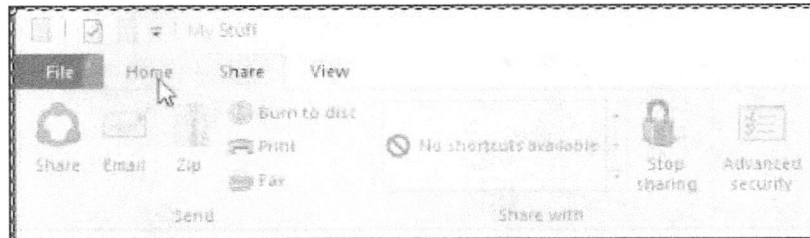

   ☐ from the list of tools at the left, click **Animations**

   ☐ from the list of Animations, drag the **Custom** animation to the **Creating Folders** group on the **Timeline**

   ☐ drag the animation aligning its left edge at **47;27**

   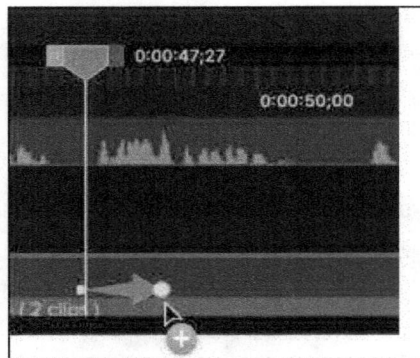

   On the Timeline, notice that the animation is represented by an arrow with two circles (one circle is at the arrowhead; the other circle is positioned at the left of the arrow). The circle on the left represents the beginning of the animation. The circle at the right represents the end of the animation. You can change the zoom percentage by selecting the tail or the head and changing the Scale on the Properties panel.

   ☐ on the **Timeline**, select the animation's head at **48;27** (the larger circle)

   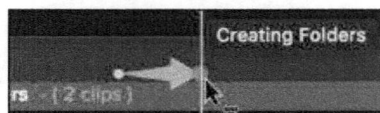

☐ on the **Properties** panel, change the **Scale** to **200**

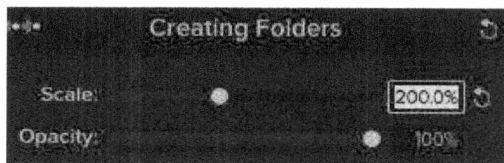

☐ on the **Canvas**, drag the video down and to the right so you can see the top left of the video

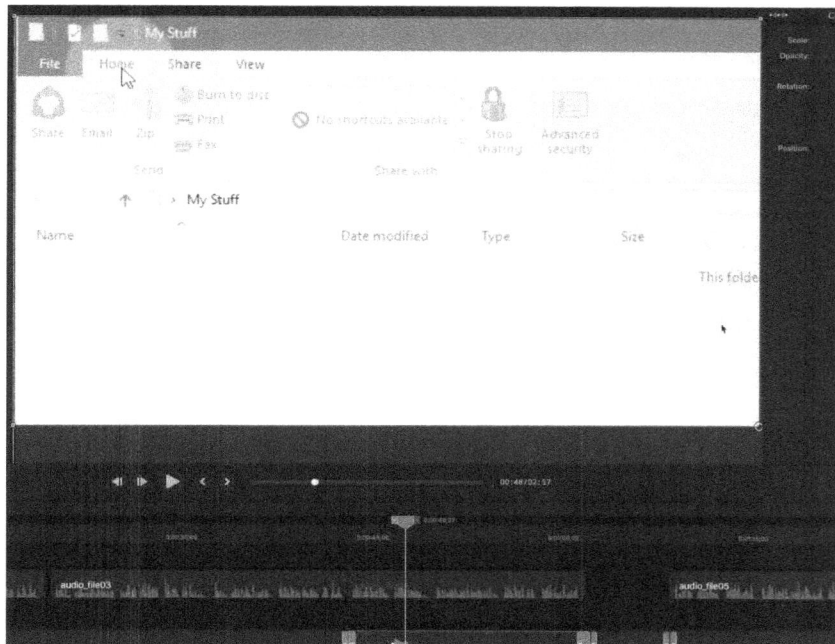

3. On the **Timeline**, position the **Playhead** a few seconds to the left of the zoom Animation you just edited.

4. Preview the project.

   Thanks to the animation, you are automatically taken closer to the action in the video.

5. Save the project and close the project.

NOTES

Markers

Markers are project-wide breadcrumbs that can be added to the Timeline or Timeline objects. Markers are the key to Camtasia's interactive features, such as a table of contents, closed captions, hotspot functionality, and quizzing.

Guided Activity 45: Add a Timeline Marker

1. Open and upgrade/convert the **MarkMe** project.

2. Add and rename a Timeline Marker.

   ☐ on the Timeline, position the Playhead at **00;25**

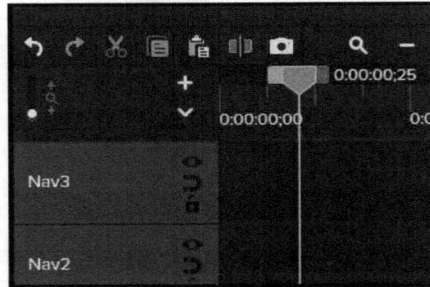

   ☐ choose **Modify > Markers > Add Timeline Marker**

On the Timeline, a marker is added just below the Playhead. On the Properties panel, the new marker is named **Marker**.

   ☐ on the **Properties** panel, change the **Marker name** to **Home** and press [**enter**]

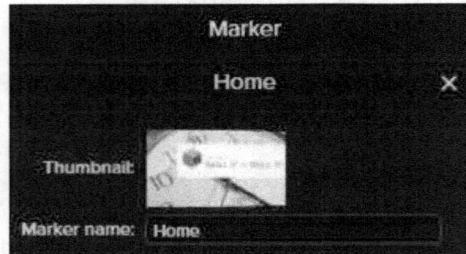

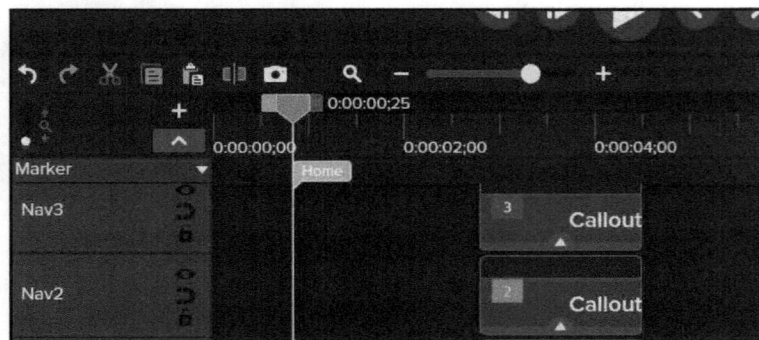

Markers and TOC Confidence Check

1. Still working in the **MarkMe** project, position the **Playhead** just after the transition for the **Lesson 1** group (05;15).

2. Add a new Timeline marker (**Modify > Markers > Add Timeline Marker**) named **Lesson 1: Creating New Folders**.

3. Position the Playhead just after the transition for the **Lesson 2** group. (01:03;28)

4. Add a new Timeline marker named **Lesson 2: Renaming Folders**.

5. Position the Playhead just after the transition for the **Lesson 3** group.

6. Add a new Timeline marker named **Lesson 3: Recycling and Restoring**. (01:45;23)

   The project should now have four markers.

TechSmith provides a hosting service called Screencast where you can upload your Camtasia and Snagit output. Screencast is especially useful if you do not have a LMS or web server where you can host your output. You will need to create an account on Screencast prior to finishing this Confidence Check. If you do not have an account, go to **https://app.screencast.com/** and set one up prior to moving to the next step.

7. Export the project to **Screencast** by choosing **Export > Screencast**.

8. Title the course **Working with Folders**.

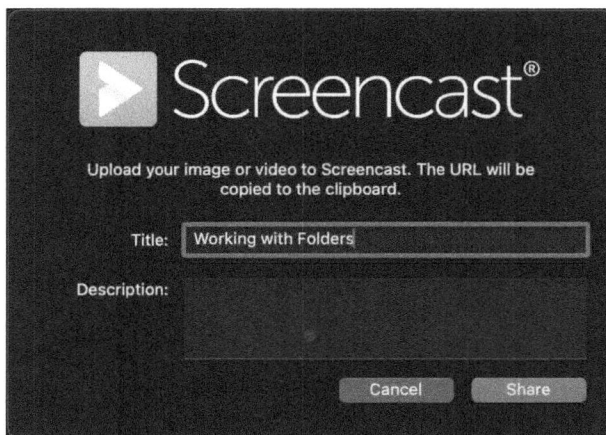

NOTES

9. Click **Export** (PC) or **Share** (Mac).

    PC users, the output should open in Screencast automatically. Mac users: Click the **Visit** button to see the output on Screencast.

    On Screencast, the Chapters can be viewed by clicking the icon on the playbar at the bottom of the lesson. On the TOC, you can click any of the menu items to jump to the Timeline markers that you added.

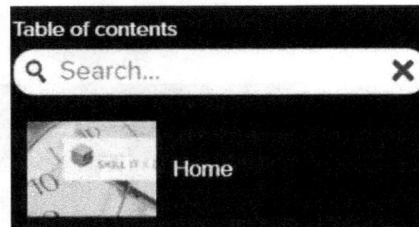

10. Close the browser and return to Camtasia.

11. Close all open windows and Save the project. (Mac users, you can save and close any open projects.)

Hotspots

To maximize the effectiveness of your eLearning videos, you can use hotspots to add interactivity. The hotspots can pause the video and wait for a click from your learner. Once clicked, a hotspot can be set up to take the learner to a marker, a website, or a specific time on the Timeline.

Guided Activity 46: Add an Interactive Hotspot

1. Open and upgrade/convert the **HotSpotMe** project.

   There are three shapes on the Canvas and at the beginning of the Timeline in the **Nav1**, **Nav2**, and **Nav3** tracks. You're going to use a hotspot to make each shape interactive.

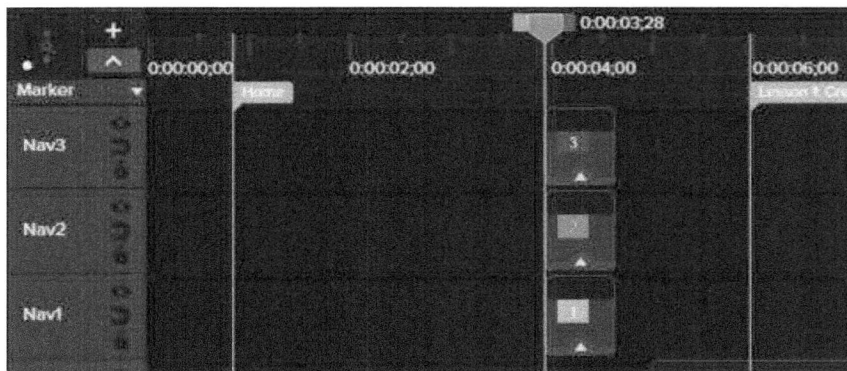

2. Add an Interactive Hotspot to an object on the Canvas.

   ☐ zoom a bit closer to the **Timeline**

   ☐ on the **Timeline**, **Nav1** track, double-click the **green shape**

   The green annotation containing the number **1** is displayed on the Canvas and selected.

   ☐ from the tools at the left, click **Visual Effects**

   ☐ right-click **Interactive Hotspot** and choose **Add to Selected Media**

NOTES

3. Add an action to a hotspot.

❒ on the **Properties** panel, **Interactive Hotspot** section, ensure **Pause at end** is selected

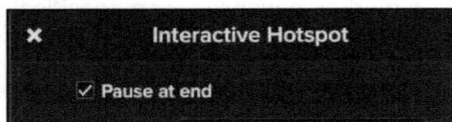

✖	Interactive Hotspot
	☑ Pause at end

This option ensures that the video doesn't move forward without giving the learner a chance to interact with the media.

❒ on the **Properties** panel, **Interactive Hotspot** section, select **Marker**

❒ from the **Marker** drop-down menu, choose the **Lesson 1: Creating New Folders** marker (you learned how to create this particular marker on page 130)

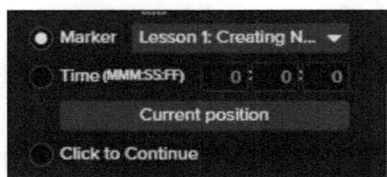

● Marker	Lesson 1: Creating N... ▼
○ Time (MMM:SS:FF)	0 : 0 : 0
	Current position
○ Click to Continue	

Interactive Hotspot Confidence Check

1. Add an Interactive Hotspot to the red annotation in the Nav2 track.

2. Make the target of the hotspot the **Lesson 2** marker.

● Marker	Lesson 2: Renaming... ▼

3. Add an Interactive Hotspot to the annotation in the Nav3 track.

4. Make the target of the hotspot the **Lesson 3** marker.

● Marker	Lesson 3: Recycling a... ▼

5. Export the project to **Screencast** with the Title: **Hotspot Version of Working with Folders**.

6. Visit the lesson on Screencast and play the video.

7. When the boxes containing 1, 2, and 3 appear onscreen, the video stops.

8. Click any of the hotspots to test the interactivity.

9. Close the browser and return to Camtasia.

10. Save the project. (Mac users, you can also close the project.)

iCONLOGiC™

Module 8: Quizzes and Reporting Results

In This Module You Will Learn About:

- Quizzes, page 136
- Reporting Quiz Results, page 142

And You Will Learn To:

- Add a Quiz to a Project, page 136
- Add a Multiple Choice Question, page 138
- Add a Fill In the Blank Question, page 139
- Create a Content Package on the PC, page 142
- Create a Content Package on the Mac, page 145

NOTES

Quizzes

In a live, instructor-led class—whether virtual or onsite—a trainer can gauge the effectiveness of a lesson by simply asking direct or overhead questions. When a trainer asks questions, learners can share what they've learned and demonstrate comprehension. You can achieve nearly the same level of learner interaction by adding a quiz to your Camtasia project.

A Camtasia quiz can contain any or all of the following question types: Multiple choice, True/False, Fill in the blank, and Short answer. Camtasia handles the appearance of quiz questions behind the scenes, and there are few options for customizing the appearance or functionality of a quiz or its questions. Regarding quiz scoring, every question you add to a quiz is scored equally. For example, if you add four quiz questions, each question is worth 25 points; if you add two questions, each is worth 50 points.

Guided Activity 47: Add a Quiz to a Project

1. Open and upgrade/convert the **QuizMe** project.

2. Add a quiz to the Timeline.

   ☐ on the **Timeline**, position the **Playhead** just after the last group (at **2:57;17**)

   ☐ choose **View > Show Quizzes**

   A Quiz Track is added along the top of the Timeline.

   ☐ position your cursor on the Quiz Track just beneath the Playhead (which you positioned at **2:57;17**

   A green plus sign appears above the cursor. The plus sign indicates the ability to add a quiz placeholder.

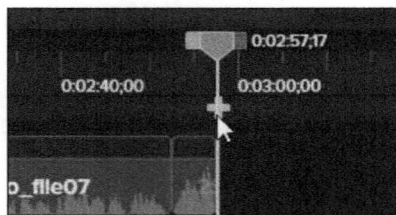

❏ click one time in the **Quiz Track** to add a quiz placeholder

By default, the quiz placeholder is named **Quiz 1**.

3. Rename the quiz.

❏ on the **Properties** panel, click **Quiz Options** (it's called **Quiz Option Properties** on the Mac, as shown in the second image below)

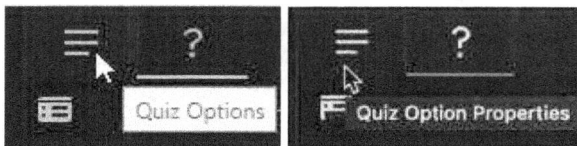

❏ change the **Quiz Name** to **Folders Quiz**

4. Ensure that the quiz will score the quiz questions.

❏ from just above the **Preview** button, ensure that **Viewers can see their results** is selected

❏ from just above the **Preview** button, ensure that **Score Quiz** is selected

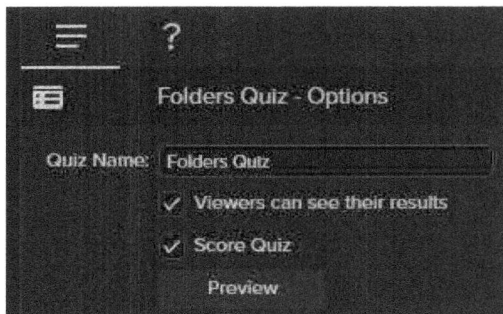

Guided Activity 48: Add a Multiple Choice Question

NOTES

1. Ensure that the **QuizMe** project is open.

2. Add a Multiple Choice question to the quiz.

   ☐ on the **Properties** panel, click **Quiz Question Properties** [?]

   ☐ from the **Type** drop-down menu, choose **Multiple Choice**

3. Type the question text.

   ☐ in the Question area, replace the placeholder text with **When giving a folder a name, how many characters can you use?**

4. Add four answers to the question.

   ☐ in the first **Answer** area, replace the placeholder text with **9**

   ☐ in the next **Answer** area, type **255**

   ☐ in the next **Answer** area, type **11**

   ☐ in the next **Answer** area, type **218**

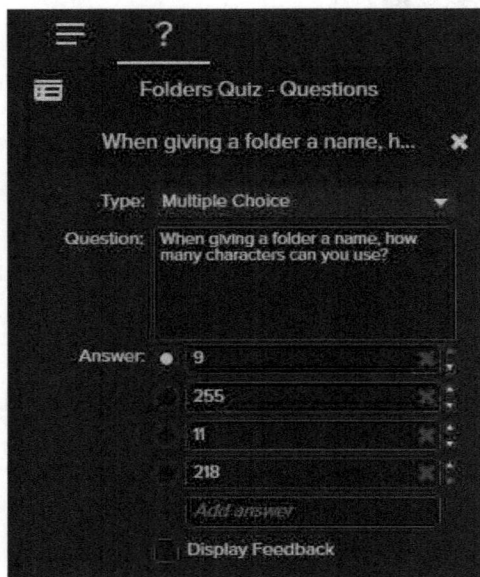

Note: There is always an extra *"Add answer"* placeholder added to the Answer area. Unless you add an answer, the extra choice will not appear in the quiz.

5. Specify a correct answer.

   ☐ click the circle to the left of the second answer, **255**

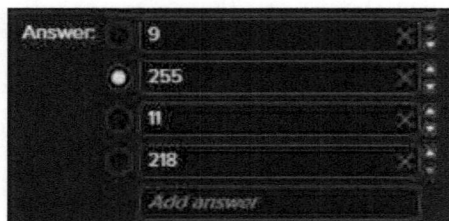

6. Save the project.

Guided Activity 49: Add a Fill In the Blank Question

1. Ensure that the **QuizMe** project is open.

2. Add a question.

   ☐ on the **Properties** panel, click **Add Question**

   Note: You may need to scroll down a bit to see the Add Question area.

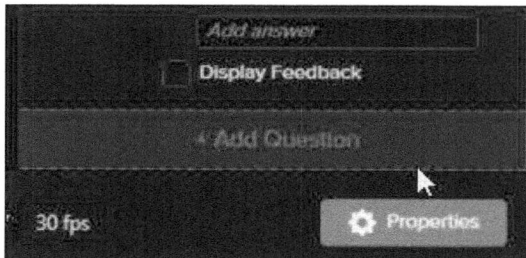

   The new question appears below the first.

3. Specify the question type.

   ☐ from the **Type** drop-down menu, choose **Fill in the Blank**

4. Edit the Question.

   ☐ replace the **Question Text** placeholder text with **The New Folder icon is found on the _____ tab of the Ribbon.**

5. Edit the Answer.

   ☐ in the **Answer** area, replace the placeholder text with **Home**

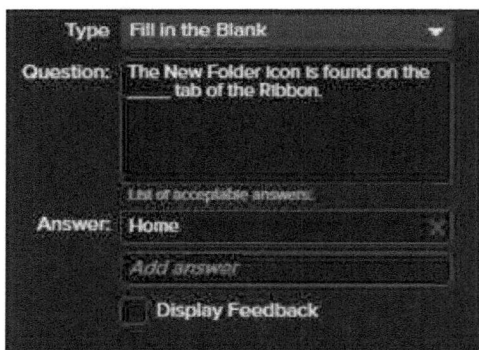

6. Save the project.

NOTES

Quiz Confidence Check

1. Preview the quiz. PC users, click the **See how Quiz looks in your viewer** icon. Mac users, click the **Preview quiz** icon.)

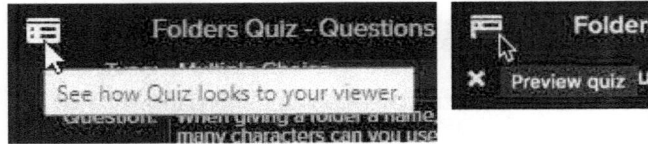

A preview of the quiz appears on the Canvas.

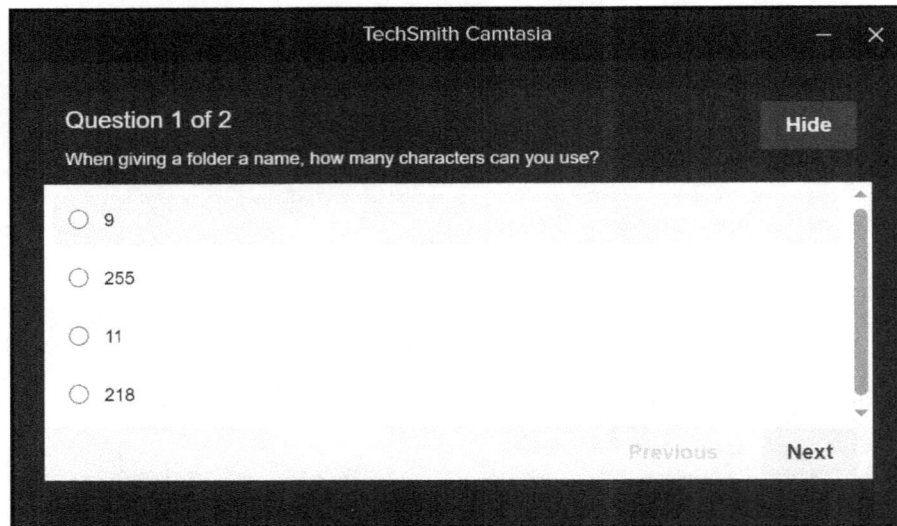

TechSmith Camtasia — ✕

Question 1 of 2   Hide

When giving a folder a name, how many characters can you use?

○ 9

○ 255

○ 11

○ 218

Previous   **Next**

2. Select any of the answers in the first question and click the **Next** button (you'll likely need to scroll down to see the Next button).

3. Type anything you'd like into the text field within the **Fill in the Blank** question and then click the **Submit Answers** button.

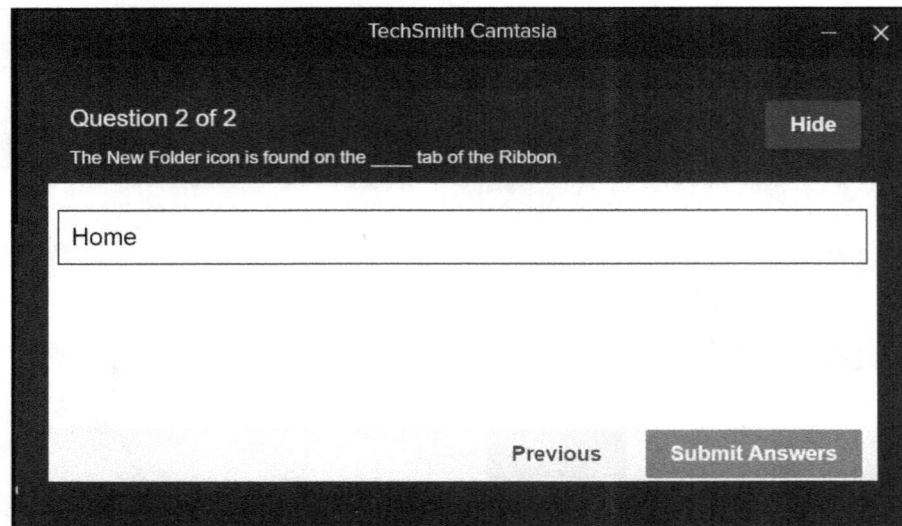

TechSmith Camtasia — ✕

Question 2 of 2   Hide

The New Folder icon is found on the _____ tab of the Ribbon.

Home

Previous   **Submit Answers**

4. Click the **View Answers** button.

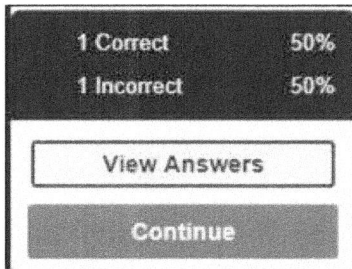

```
1 Correct        50%
1 Incorrect      50%

View Answers

Continue
```

Correct answers are shown with a green check mark. Wrong answers are flagged with a red X.

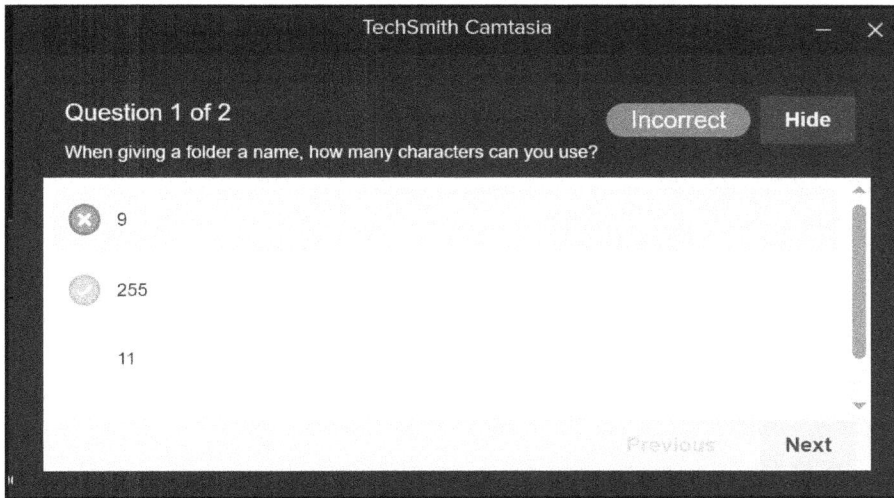

```
TechSmith Camtasia                                    —    ✕

Question 1 of 2                        Incorrect      Hide
When giving a folder a name, how many characters can you use?

  ✕  9

  ✓  255

     11

                                       Previous      Next
```

5. Close the Quiz preview.

6. Save the project. (Mac users, you can also close the project.)

NOTES

Reporting Quiz Results

To track quiz results, most eLearning developers upload their Camtasia eLearning courses to a Learning Management System (LMS). At a minimum, an LMS tracks learner access to the content, delivery of the content, and student performance through tracking and reporting. Camtasia projects can be configured to report quiz scores to an LMS.

SCORM

SCORM, which stands for Sharable Content Object Reference Model, is a set of standards developed by both public- and private-sector organizations to ensure eLearning content can be shared and reused across different systems. Originally initiated by the U.S. Department of Defense through the Advanced Distributed Learning (ADL) Initiative, SCORM defines how online learning content is packaged, launched, and tracked within a Learning Management System (LMS). By following SCORM standards, developers can create courses that are compatible with any SCORM-compliant LMS, making it easier to deliver, manage, and report on learner progress and performance.

Courses and LMSs that adhere to SCORM specifications enable the seamless sharing and reuse of content across organizations, including federal agencies, colleges, and universities. While SCORM is not the only eLearning standard available, it remains one of the most widely used. Camtasia supports the two primary versions of SCORM: version 1.2, released in 1999, and SCORM 2004.

Manifests

A manifest file enables your exported eLearning to be launched from a SCORM-compliant LMS. When you export a Camtasia project, you can have Camtasia automatically generate this manifest file for you. The file contains XML tags that describe the organization and structure of your published project, allowing the LMS to properly interpret and track it.

In the following activities, you'll create a SCORM-compliant content package—including a manifest file—suitable for upload into any SCORM-compliant LMS. Because the export process differs significantly between PC and Mac, the instructions are divided. PC users, you're up first. Mac users, skip to page 145 for your step-by-step guide.

Guided Activity 50: Create a Content Package on the PC

1. Open and upgrade/convert the **ReportMe** project.

   At the far right of the **Quiz Track** of the Timeline, notice that this project includes a quiz.

2. Enable SCORM reporting.

   ❏ choose **Export > Local File**

   ❏ from the **File type** drop-down menu, choose **MP4 with Smart Player**

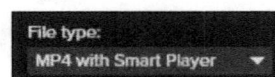

   File type:
   MP4 with Smart Player ▼

   ❏ expand **Advanced Settings**

   ⌄ Advanced Settings

❑ select the **Smart Player** tab

❑ select **Report using SCORM**

Dimensions	Encoding	Audio	Smart Player
✓ Report using SCORM			SCORM Options...

3. Set up the Manifest file.

❑ at the right of **Report using SCORM**, click **SCORM Options**   SCORM Options...

The Manifest Options dialog box opens.

❑ change the **Version** to **1.2**

Version	1.2	▼

Some LMSs support SCORM version 1.2; some support only 2004, while others support both. Although it's typically a safe bet to go with SCORM 1.2, discuss the ideal version with your LMS vendor.

❑ leave the **Identifier** unchanged

Identifier	ID-b7ef5973-cfc8-49a1-8896-f8c0fe03c082

Some LMSs require a specific course Identifier. However, in my experience creating content packages over the years, I've rarely needed to change this value. Only consider modifying it if you are specifically instructed to do so by your LMS administrator.

❑ change the Course information **Title** to **Computer Basics**

❑ add the following **Description** text: **This course will teach you everything you ever wanted to know about computers but were afraid to ask.**

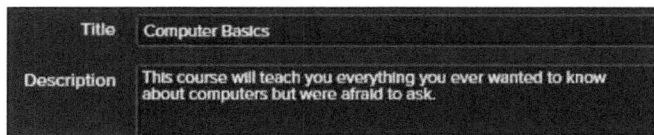

Title	Computer Basics
Description	This course will teach you everything you ever wanted to know about computers but were afraid to ask.

❑ change the Lesson Information **Title** to **Creating, Renaming, and Recycling Folders**

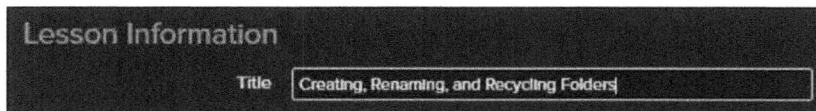

Lesson Information

Title	Creating, Renaming, and Recycling Folders

When I create my courses, they typically consist of multiple lessons. While it's possible to create a single Camtasia project and treat it as both the course and the lesson, it's far more common to develop a course and then add several lessons. Each lesson is a standalone Camtasia project.

The project you worked on during the activities and confidence checks led to the Creating, Renaming, and Recycling lesson. Moving forward, you could create additional lessons for the Computer Basics course. Each new lesson would use the same course title

NOTES

NOTES

("Computer Basics") for the course information but have a unique lesson title. By using the same course title for each lesson, most LMSs will automatically group the lessons into the correct course when you upload the content package.

❑ from the **Quiz success** area, set the **Passing Score** to **50%**

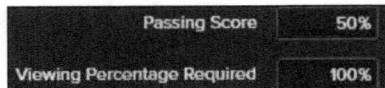

Passing Score	50%
Viewing Percentage Required	100%

You have only two questions in the quiz, so a 50% pass setting seems about right.

❑ click the **OK** button

You should be back on the Export Local File screen.

❑ click the **Export** button

4. Once the export process is complete, click the **Open file location** button.

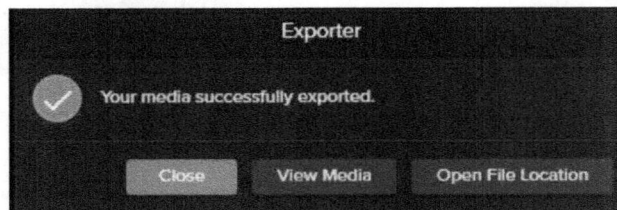

Exporter

✓ Your media successfully exported.

Close   View Media   Open File Location

The zipped content package has been created, ready for you to upload into any SCORM-compliant LMS.

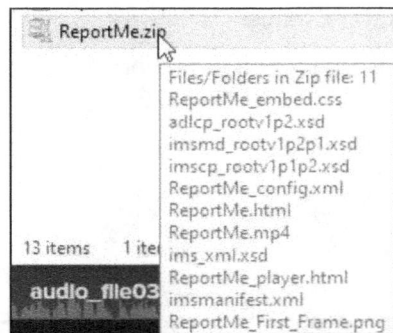

ReportMe.zip

Files/Folders in Zip file: 11
ReportMe_embed.css
adlcp_rootv1p2.xsd
imsmd_rootv1p2p1.xsd
imscp_rootv1p1p2.xsd
ReportMe_config.xml
ReportMe.html
ReportMe.mp4
ims_xml.xsd
ReportMe_player.html
imsmanifest.xml
ReportMe_First_Frame.png

13 items   1 ite
audio_file03

5. Close all windows.

The remaining steps in this module are for Mac users. You can move to the "PowerPoint, Captions, and Templates" module which begins on page 147.

Guided Activity 51: Create a Content Package on the Mac

1. Ensure that the **ReportMe** project is still open.

2. Enable SCORM reporting.

   ☐ choose **Export > Local File**

   ☐ from beneath the **Caption Style** area, ensure **Include Quiz** is selected

   ☐ from beneath the **Caption Style** area, select **Include SCORM**

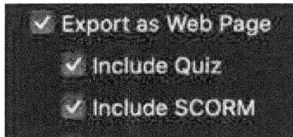

   ☑ Export as Web Page
      ☑ Include Quiz
      ☑ Include SCORM

3. Set up the Manifest file.

   ☐ to the right of **Include SCORM**, click the **Options** button

   The Manifest Options dialog box opens.

   ☐ change the **Course Title** to **Computer Basics**

   ☐ add the following **Description** text: **This course will teach you everything you ever wanted to know about computers but were afraid to ask.**

   ☐ change the **SCORM version** to **1.2**

Course Information:	
Identifier:	ID-E1FFC1AC-971B-4E36-A162-2E2EC100A7BD
Title:	Computer Basics
Description:	This course will teach you everything you ever wanted to know about computers but were afraid to ask.
Subject:	
Version:	1.2
Language:	en Duration: 00:02:57.57 hh:mm:ss

   Some LMSs support SCORM version 1.2; some support only 2004, while others support both. Although it's typically a safe bet to go with SCORM 1.2, discuss the ideal version with your LMS vendor.

   ☐ change the **Lesson Title** to **Creating, Renaming, and Recycling Folders**

   When I create my courses, those courses consist of multiple lessons. Indeed, you can create a single Camtasia project and treat that project as both the course and the lesson. However, it is far more common to develop a course and add several lessons. Each lesson is a standalone Camtasia project.

   The project you worked on during the activities and confidence checks led to the Creating, Renaming, and Recycling lesson. Moving forward, you could create additional lessons for

NOTES

NOTES

the Computer Basics course. Each new lesson would use the same title (Computer Basics) for the course information but have a unique lesson title. If you use the same course title for each lesson, most LMSs automatically group the lessons into the correct course when you upload the content package.

❏ from the **Quiz Success** area, set the Passing Score to **50%**

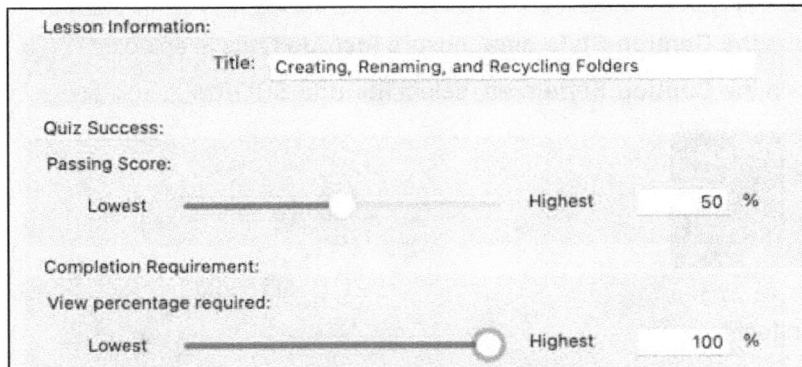

You have only two questions in your quiz, so a 50% pass setting seems about right.

❏ from the **SCORM Package options** area, select **Produce zip file**

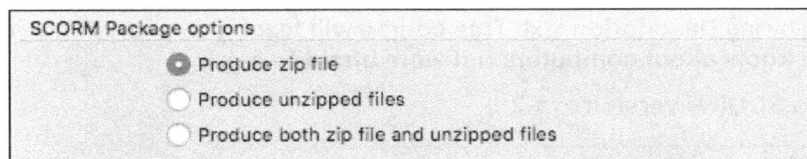

❏ click the **OK** button

❏ click the **Export** button

4. Once the Export process is complete, click the **Reveal in Finder** button.

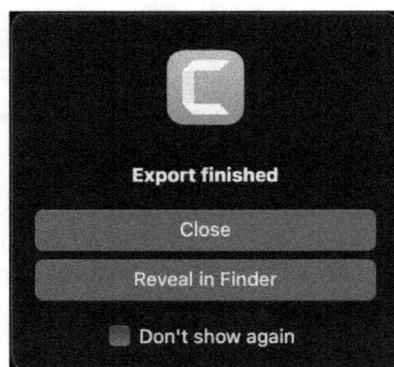

The zipped content package has been created, ready for you to upload into an LMS.

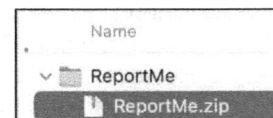

5. Close all windows.

6. Back in Camtasia, save and close the project.

iCONLOGiC™

Module 9: PowerPoint, Captions, and Templates

In This Module You Will Learn About:

And You Will Learn To:

NOTES

PowerPoint to Camtasia

I frequently meet eLearning developers who have created excellent Microsoft PowerPoint presentations and want to turn those presentations into eLearning. Unfortunately, PowerPoint on its own can't track quiz scores, create SCORM packages, or automatically upload content to platforms like YouTube or Screencast.

Rather than recreate the entire presentation from scratch in Camtasia, you have two great ways to re-purpose existing PowerPoint content.

PC users can record a PowerPoint presentation directly from within PowerPoint using the Camtasia Add-in. The finished recording is automatically added to a Camtasia project as a video on the Timeline. From there, you can enhance the project with all the Camtasia features you've been learning throughout this book.

Mac users, on the other hand, don't have access to the Camtasia Add-in for PowerPoint, as it's only available on Windows. However, you can work around this limitation by recording your presentation using Camtasia's screen recorder (you learned how to use the Recorder on page 28).

Another option—available to both Mac and PC users—is to import some or all of your PowerPoint slides into Camtasia as images. Once imported into Camtasia, the slides can be added to the Timeline and treated like any other media.

You'll explore both options—recording with the PowerPoint Add-in and importing slides as images—during the following activities.

> **Note:** The next activity is for PC users only because the Camtasia add-in is not available on the Mac. **Mac users**, you can skip ahead to the activity on page 151.

Guided Activity 52: Record PowerPoint on the PC

1. If Camtasia is running, close the program.

2. Open a PowerPoint presentation with Microsoft PowerPoint.

   ☐ using **Microsoft PowerPoint**, open **S3_Policies** from the **Camtasia 2025 Book Assets > Other_Assets** folder

Note: The Camtasia PowerPoint Add-in is automatically installed on your computer when you install the Camtasia application. Unless the Add-in has been disabled or the alert disabled, you should see the dialog box shown at the right when opening PowerPoint. To confirm that the Camtasia Add-in is installed and active, go to **File > Options > Add-ins** from within PowerPoint.

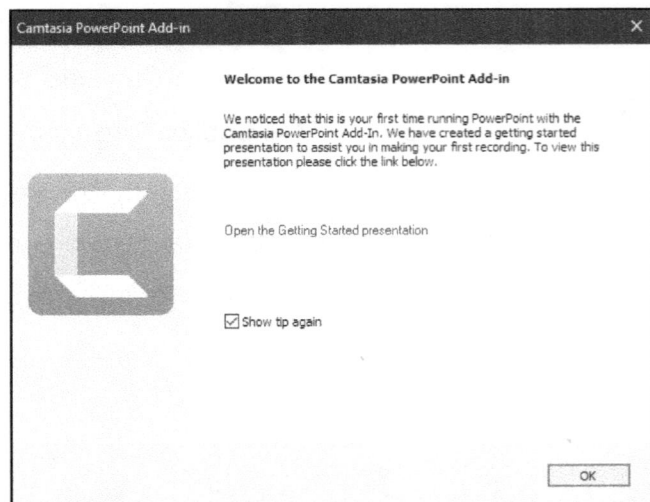

Camtasia PowerPoint Add-in

Welcome to the Camtasia PowerPoint Add-in

We noticed that this is your first time running PowerPoint with the Camtasia PowerPoint Add-In. We have created a getting started presentation to assist you in making your first recording. To view this presentation please click the link below.

Open the Getting Started presentation

☑ Show tip again

OK

❑ click the **OK** button

3. Review the Camtasia PowerPoint tools.

❑ on the **PowerPoint Ribbon**, click the **Add-Ins** tab

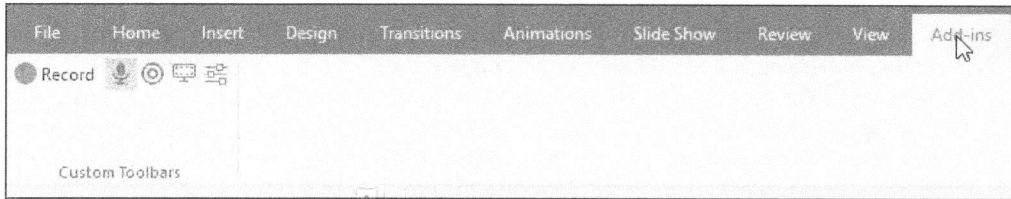

Camtasia recording tools appear at the left of the Add-ins tab.

4. Record the PowerPoint presentation.

❑ from the **Custom Toolbars** area, click the **Record** tool

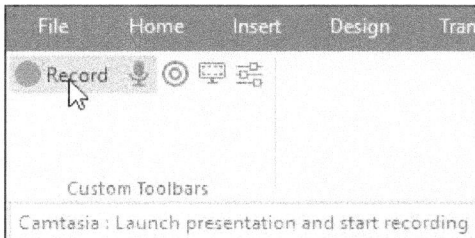

The PowerPoint slide show begins.

❑ in the lower right screen, click the **Click to begin recording** button

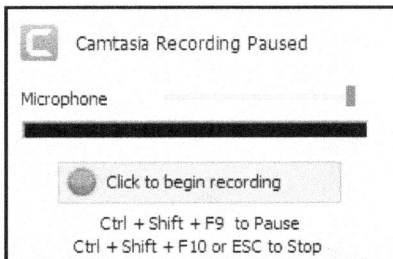

At this point, the presentation is being recorded, much like your screen was recorded when you learned to use the Camtasia Recorder (on page 28).

❑ take your time and click in the middle of each slide to progress through the slide show

When you reach the end of the slide show, the alert dialog box shown below appears.

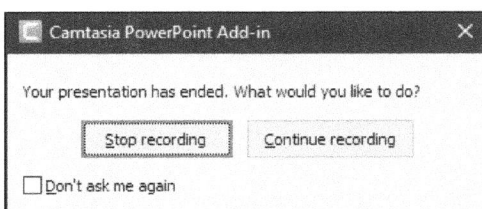

NOTES

❏ click the **Stop Recording** button

You are prompted to save the recording.

❏ navigate to the **Camtasia 2025 Book Assets** folder

❏ open the **Video Files** folder and then save the file

You will be asked if you'd like to **Produce your recording** or **Edit your recording**. The former will take you directly to the Export options where you can elect to produce the video for Screencast, for YouTube, or as HTML5. The latter opens the recording in the Camtasia Editor where you can enhance the video using any of the production techniques you've learned to add during the lessons throughout this book (add annotations, audio, quizzes, behaviors, images, videos, etc.).

❏ select **Edit your recording**

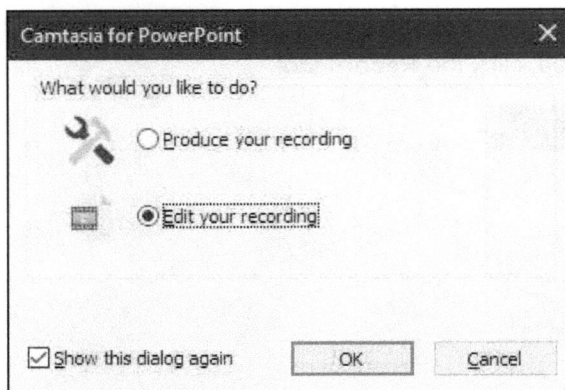

❏ click the **OK** button

The PowerPoint presentation is added to the Camtasia Media Bin.

❏ right-click the recording and choose **Add to Timeline at Playhead**.

You will be prompted to import the PowerPoint Slide Notes as captions. You'll learn about captions shortly. For this activity, the captions are not needed.

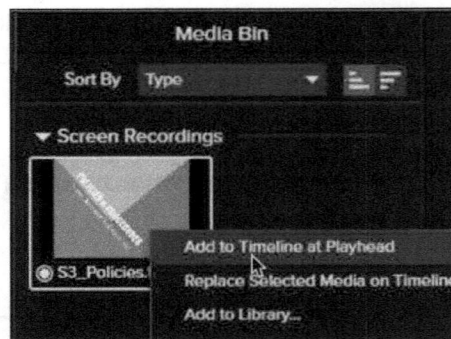

❏ click **No**

The recording is added to the Timeline. At this point, you could add audio, a quiz, and other Camtasia assets as you have learned to do throughout this book.

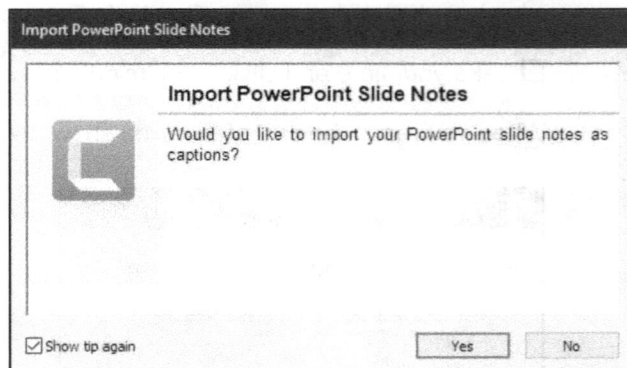

Guided Activity 53: Import a PowerPoint Presentation

1. **All users:** Create a new Camtasia project (there is no need to save previous projects).

2. Import PowerPoint slides into Camtasia as images.

   ❑ choose **File > Import > Media**

   ❑ from **Camtasia 2025 Book Assets > Other_Assets**, open **S3_Policies**

   The PowerPoint slides are automatically added to the Media Bin as individual images. **Mac users,** you'll likely see three dialog boxes. Two asking for permission that will allow Camtasia access to the Documents folder. A third dialog box prompts you to import all of the slides or select from a range of slides. Click the **Allow** button when prompted and then click the **Import** button.

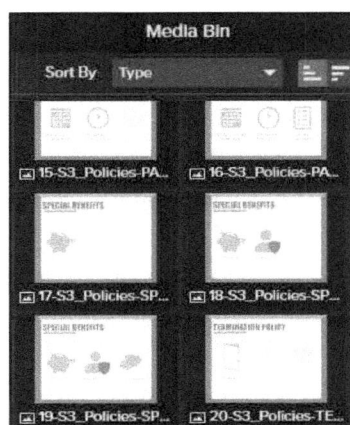

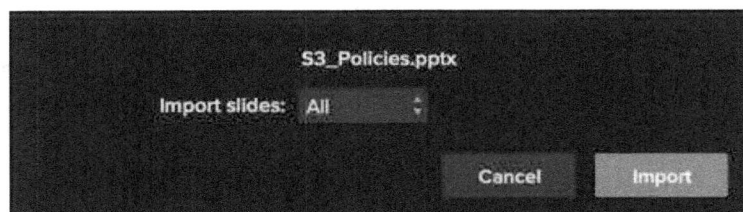

3. Add multiple images to the Timeline at one time.

   ❑ on the **Media Bin**, select any one of the images

   ❑ PC users, press [**ctrl**] [**a**] to select all of the images;
   Mac users, press [**command**] [**a**] to select all of the images

   ❑ right-click any of one of the selected images and choose **Add to Timeline at Playhead**

4. Mac users, close the project without saving. PC users, leave the project open. During the next activity, you'll be prompted to save the project while opening another. There is no need to save it.

NOTES

Closed Captions

If your project includes audio and your learners cannot hear it—whether due to a disability or hardware limitations—consider adding closed captions. These captions typically match the voiceover audio in your Camtasia project and provide essential accessibility.

There are several ways to add closed captions to a Camtasia project:

- ☐ Manually type what you hear by listening to the Timeline audio
- ☐ Copy and paste from a script
- ☐ Use Speech-to-Text (available to PC users only)
- ☐ Import an SRT file
- ☐ Try the new Dynamic Closed Captions feature

If you have access to the original voiceover script, copying and pasting text into captions—one at a time—is a simple and accurate workflow.

While Speech-to-Text sounds ideal, my experience with the feature has been mixed. I've consistently needed to review and significantly edit the automatically generated text.

Dynamic Closed Captions, a newer AI-powered feature, can automatically generate visually appealing captions. It's a promising tool, though still evolving and likely to improve with future updates.

When adding captions, three factors are key: your effort, the timing of each caption, and the accuracy of the text. Of all the workflows, copying and pasting from a voiceover script is the one I most recommend. Another great option is importing SubRip (SRT) files. These raw closed caption files contain both the spoken text and corresponding timing.

Services like Rev.com allow you to upload audio files and, for around $1.50 per minute, return SRT files ready for download. You can then import the SRTs into Camtasia, where they're quickly synced with the audio on the Timeline.

Because the captioning process differs slightly between Windows and Mac, I've split up the steps. PC users, your captioning activities begin below. Mac users, you can skip ahead to page 162.

Guided Activity 54: Manually Create PC Closed Captions

1. Open and upgrade/convert the **CaptionMe** project. (PC users, when prompted to save the project from the last activity, there is no need to do so.)

   In the Voiceover track, notice that there are seven audio files track.

2. Open the Captions tool.

   - ☐ choose **View > Tools > Captions > Closed Captions**

3. Add captions manually.

   - ☐ on the **Timeline**, position the **Playhead** at **5;00** (this is where the first voiceover audio clip is positioned)
   - ☐ on the **Canvas**, click the **Play** button and listen to the audio

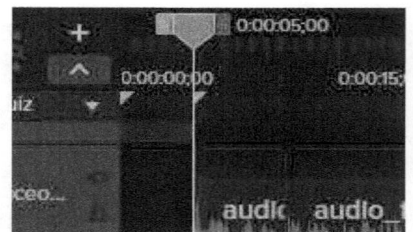

In this first audio segment, the narrator says: "Welcome to Super Simplistic Solutions learning series. This is lesson one: Creating New Folders."

❑ on the **Timeline**, re-position the **Playhead** at exactly **5;00**

❑ on the **Captions** panel, click **Add Caption**

A callout is added to both Track 4 and the Canvas.

❑ on the **Canvas**, type the following into the Caption area:
Welcome to Super Simplistic Solutions learning series.

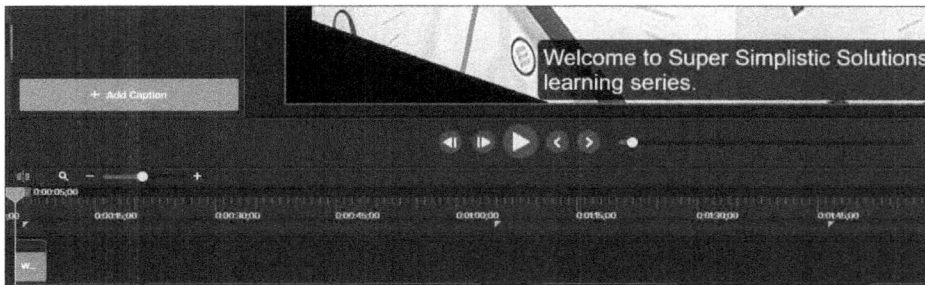

4. Format the Caption text.

❑ click the **Font Properties** drop-down menu and change the **Size** to **24**

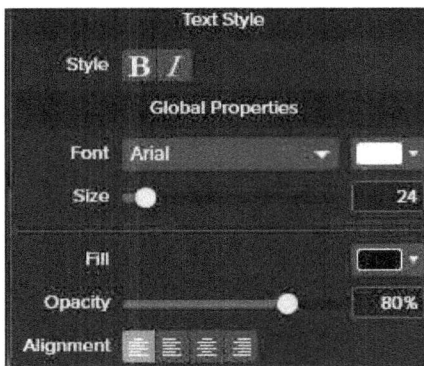

The Americans with Disabilities Act (ADA), a 1990 U.S. civil rights law, prohibits discrimination against individuals with disabilities. Generally speaking, the ADA ensures that people with disabilities have the same rights and opportunities as everyone else. The law guarantees equal opportunity for individuals with disabilities in public accommodations, employment, transportation, state and local government services, website experiences, and eLearning.

When creating eLearning content, you should avoid doing anything in your project that does not conform to ADA standards. In the image below, the caption font size is not ADA-compliant, as indicated by the X to the right of the Font Properties drop-down menu.

NOTES

5. Make Caption font formatting ADA-compliant.

☐ click the **ADA Compliance** drop-down menu

☐ click the **Make Compliant** button

The Caption's formatting now conforms to ADA standards as indicated by the check mark.

6. Add another Caption.

☐ on the **Timeline**, position the Playhead just to the right of the first caption

☐ from the **Captions** panel, click the **Add Caption** button

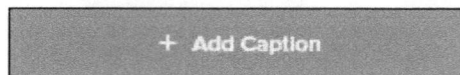

☐ in the Caption area on the Canvas, type **This is lesson one: Creating New Folders.**

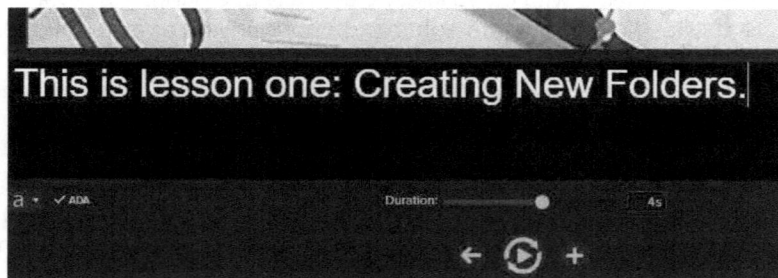

Guided Activity 55: Control PC Caption Timing

1. Ensure that the **CaptionMe** project is open.

2. Zoom closer to the Timeline.

3. On the **Timeline**, notice that the first caption is onscreen about a second and a half too long. The vertical line in the image below indicates when the narrator has finished saying the word "series."

It's a best practice to synchronize the audio and the timing of the captions. In this instance, you need to shorten the caption's playtime.

4. Adjust caption timing.

☐ on the **Timeline**, drag the **right** edge of the **first** caption to the **left** a bit to shorten its play time

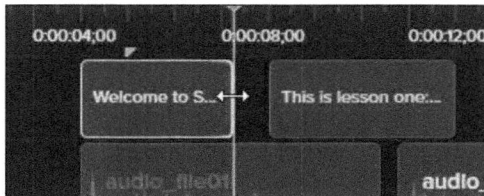

NOTES

NOTES

PC Captions Confidence Check

1. Move the second caption left so it lines up with the audio as shown below.

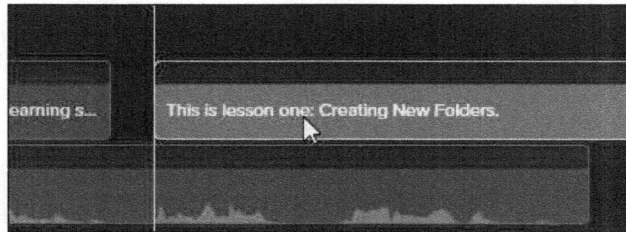

2. Shorten the playtime of the second caption so it matches the audio.

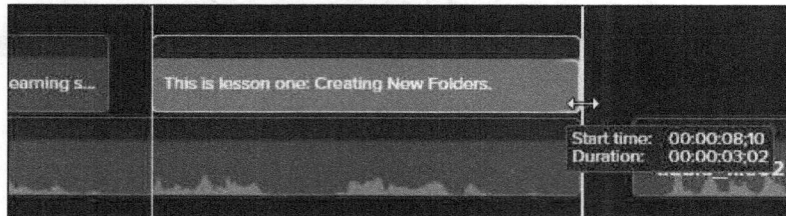

3. Add a third caption just to the right of the first two containing this text: **This lesson is going to teach you how to create a new folder on your computer.**

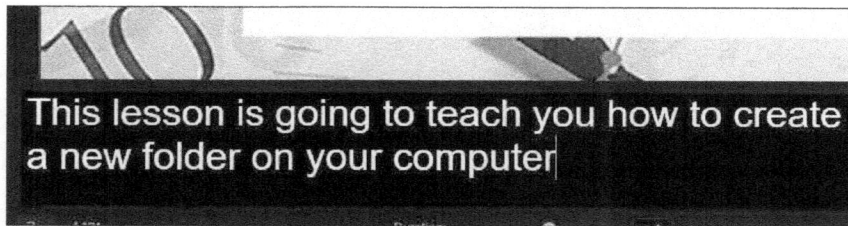

4. If necessary, make adjustments to the caption's timing so it matches the audio as closely as possible.

5. Export the project as a **Local File**, **MP4 with Smart Player**.

6. Once the export process is complete, **View** the media in your browser.

   Notice that a CC button has been automatically added to the Player.

7. On the Player, click the **CC** button to view the captions.

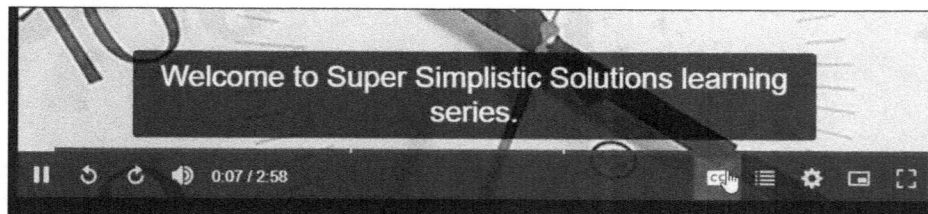

8. Close the browser window.

9. Minimize Camtasia and, from the **Camtasia 2025 Book Assets**, **Other_Assets** folder, open **CreatingFoldersVoiceoverScript** using Microsoft Word.

> ## Audio File 1:
> Welcome to Super Simplistic Solutions learning series.
> This is lesson one: Creating New Folders.
>
> ## Audio File 2:
> This lesson is going to teach you how to create a new folder on your computer, how to rename it, and how to both delete and restore recycled items.
>
> ## Audio File 3:
> When creating folders keep in mind that you can create as many folders as you need.

10. In the **Audio File 2** text section, select **"how to rename it, and how to both delete and restore recycled items"** and copy the text to the Clipboard.

11. Return to Camtasia and the **CaptionMe** project.

12. Position the Playhead just to the right of your existing captions.

13. Create a new caption and paste the text you copied into the space beneath the Canvas.

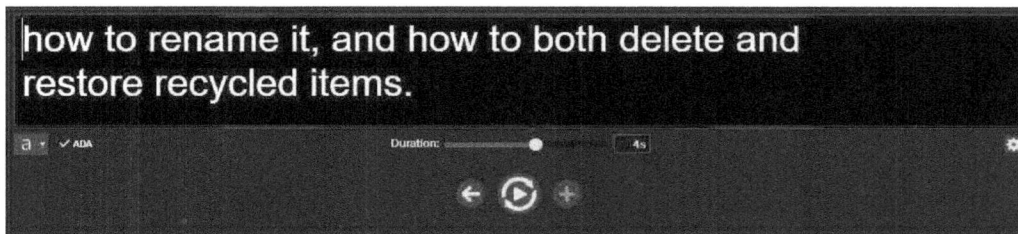

14. Save the project.

|NOTES|

Guided Activity 56: Use Speech-to-Text to Create Captions

1. Ensure that the **CaptionMe** project is open.

2. Remove a track and its media.

   ☐ on the **Timeline**, right-click **Track 4** and choose **Remove Track**

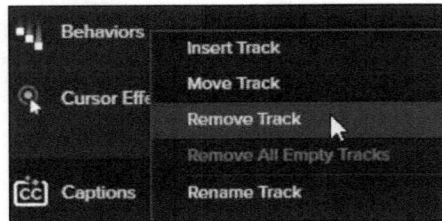

   Because there is media on the track, you are prompted to confirm the action.

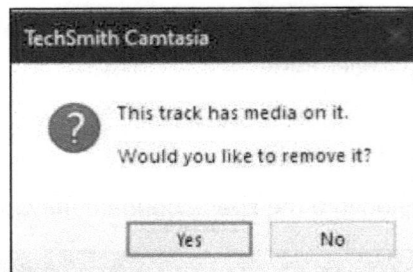

   ☐ click the **Yes** button

3. Create captions using Speech-to-Text.

   ☐ from the upper left of the **Captions** panel, click **Script Options** ⚙

   ☐ choose **Speech-to-Text**

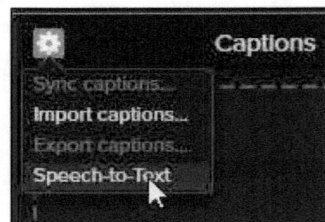

   Camtasia "listens" to the voiceover audio in the background and, like magic, creates Captions on a new Track 4.

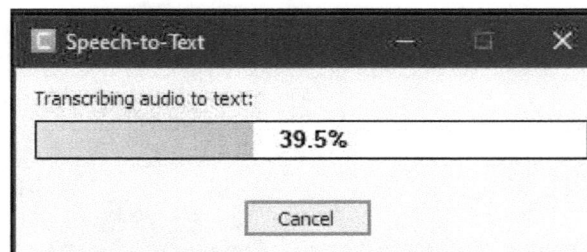

Look through the Timeline and notice in the image below that although much of the audio was transcribed nicely, many of the captions need editing.

[MUSIC] Welcome to super simplistic

You've now learned three ways to create Captions: transcribing, copy/paste from a script, and Speech-to-Text. Now let's see how well SRTs work.

NOTES

Guided Activity 57: Import Captions on the PC

1. Ensure that the **CaptionMe** project is open.

2. Remove a track and its media.

   ☐ on the **Timeline**, right-click **Track 4** and choose **Remove Track**

   Because there is once again media on the track, you are prompted to confirm the action.

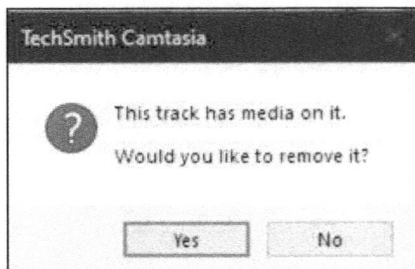

   ☐ click the **Yes** button

3. Import a caption.

   ☐ choose **File > Import > Captions**

   ☐ from **Camtasia 2025 Book Assets > Audio Files > SRT Files**, open **audio_file01.srt**

   The caption is added to Track 4. Because the SRT file contains the voiceover script text *and* the timing, the playtime of the caption is an exact match for the audio_file01 media in the voiceover track.

4. Reposition a caption on the Timeline.

   ☐ on the **Timeline**, drag the caption in Track 4 until its **left edge** aligns with the **audio_file01** media in the Voiceover track

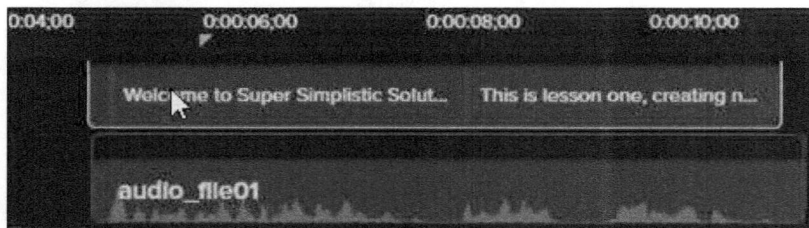

   You have learned multiple ways to create captions: transcribing, copy/paste from a script, Speech-to-Text, and importing. Camtasia offers one more feature for adding captions: Dynamic Captions, which you will learn about next.

Guided Activity 58: Create Dynamic Captions on the PC

1. Ensure that the **CaptionMe** project is open.

2. Remove Track 4.

3. Open the Dynamic Captions tool.

   ❏ choose **View > Tools > Captions > Dynamic Captions**

   The Dynamic Caption Styles open.

4. Add Dynamic Captions.

   ❏ from the **Dynamic Caption Styles** area, select any style that you like

   ❏ **drag** the dynamic caption style onto the Timeline (just above the Voiceover Audio track)

   A track is added and captions are created for all of the audio files in the Voiceover Audio track. (Note that this process can take some time.)

   ❏ on the **Timeline**, drag the Dynamic Caption media left to align with the first audio file in the Voiceover Audio track

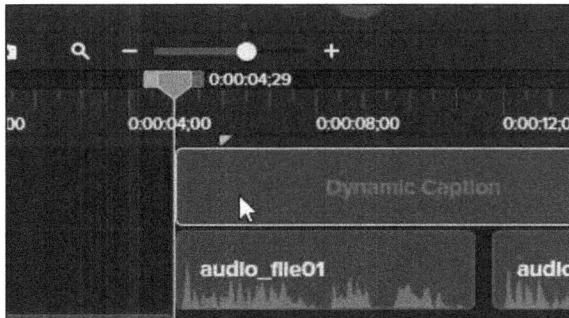

5. On the Canvas, preview the video to see the dynamic captions.

   Note: You can change the appearance of the captions on the Properties panel. And you can edit the captions onscreen by clicking the audio media. In the image below, the word "folder" was incorrectly added as "folds." It's simple enough to edit the text as needed.

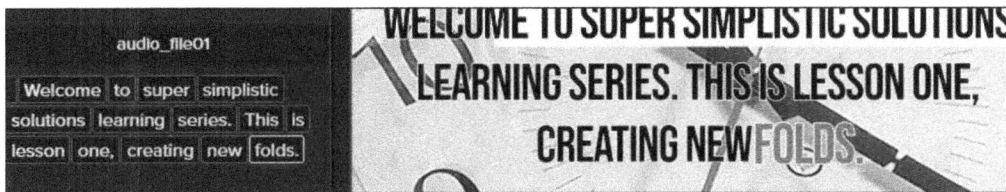

6. Save the project.

   The next few activities on Captions are for Mac users. PC users, you can skip ahead to page 172 and learn about Templates.

NOTES

Guided Activity 59: Create Mac Closed Captions

1. Mac users, save and close any open projects.

2. Open the **CaptionMe** project.

   There are several audio clips in the Voiceover track. You're going to listen to some of the clips and create a few captions.

3. Open the Captions tool.

   ❏ choose **View > Tools > Captions > Closed Captions**

4. Add captions manually.

   ❏ drag the **Captions** tool to the first audio clip in the Voiceover Track

The Caption track opens just above the Timeline.

❏ on the **Caption track**, click the **left side** of the audio waveform

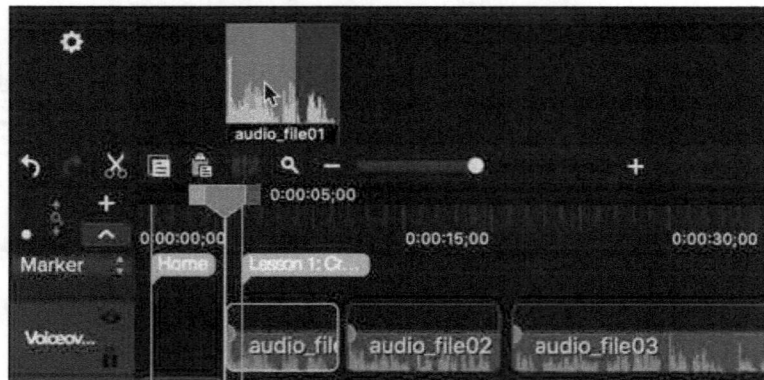

The first part of the audio plays and a typing area opens. In this first audio segment, the narrator says: **Welcome to Super Simplistic Solutions learning series. This is lesson one: Creating New Folders.**

❏ type the following into the space beneath the background image: **Welcome to Super Simplistic Solutions learning series.**

The caption you typed also appears on the Canvas. This is what learners will see if they view the lesson's closed captions.

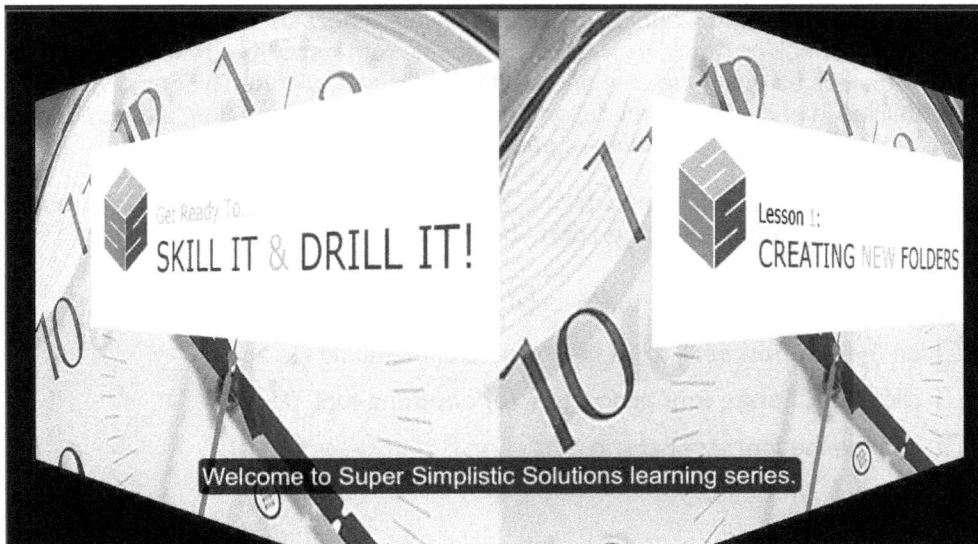

5. Format the Caption text.

❏ on the **Caption track**, double-click the left side of the caption

❏ on the caption, click the **Change font properties for captions** tool

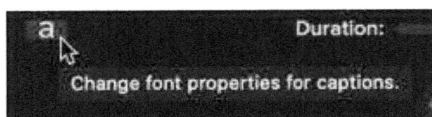

The Font options open.

NOTES

❑ change the font size to **18**

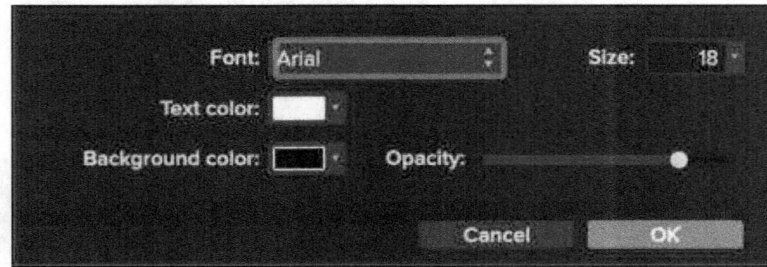

❑ click the **OK** button

On the Canvas, the change to the font size is immediate. Although the smaller font size might look better than the larger font, keep in mind that the closed captions aren't necessarily for you—they're typically meant to help learners who cannot hear the audio. When creating eLearning content, you'll need to be alert for anything you might do in your project that does not conform to the Americans with Disabilities Act (ADA).

In case you're not familiar with the ADA, it's a 1990 US civil rights law that prohibits discrimination against individuals with disabilities in all areas of public life, including jobs, schools, transportation, and all public and private places open to the general public. Generally speaking, the law ensures that people with disabilities have the same rights and opportunities as everyone else and guarantees equal opportunity for individuals with disabilities in public accommodations, employment, transportation, state and local government services, and even eLearning.

Regarding font sizes used in captions, a larger font is preferred because it is easier to see and read on a computer screen or mobile device.

6. Restore the caption's font size to its larger size.

   ❑ on the **Caption** track, click the left side of the audio file again

   ❑ click the **Change font properties for captions** tool

   ❑ change the font size back to **32**

   ❑ click the **OK** button

7. Add another caption.

   ❑ on the **Caption track**, click the **right** side of the audio waveform

   ❑ type **This is lesson one: Creating New Folders.**

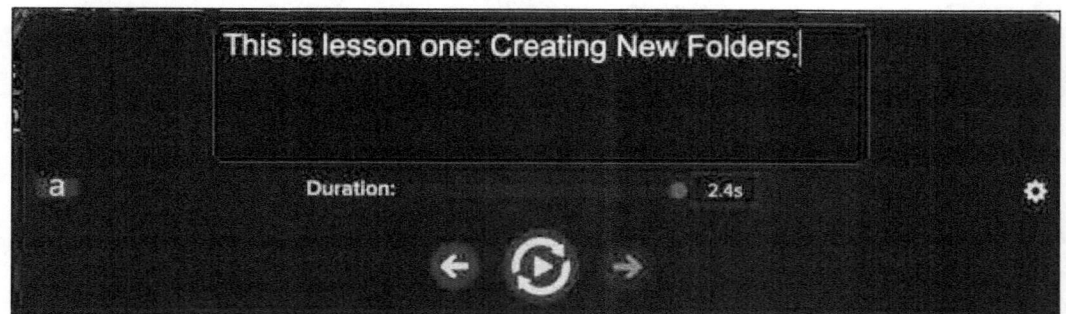

8. Preview the project from the beginning of the Timeline.

The captions appear, but they do not exactly match the voiceover audio. For instance, the first caption is onscreen a bit too long. You'll fix that next.

NOTES

Guided Activity 60: Control Mac Caption Timing

1. Ensure that the **CaptionMe.cmproj** project is open.

2. Adjust caption timing.

   ☐ on the **Caption track**, click the **left side** of the audio file

   ☐ on the Caption panel, change the **Duration** to **3** seconds

   > Welcome to Super Simplistic Solutions learning series.
   >
   > a   Duration: ●   3.0s   ⚙

3. Preview the project from the beginning of the Timeline.

   The timing for the caption is now more in sync with the voiceover audio.

Mac Captions Confidence Check

1. Add a caption to the second audio file on the **Timeline** with the following text: **This lesson is going to teach you how to create a new folder on your computer.**

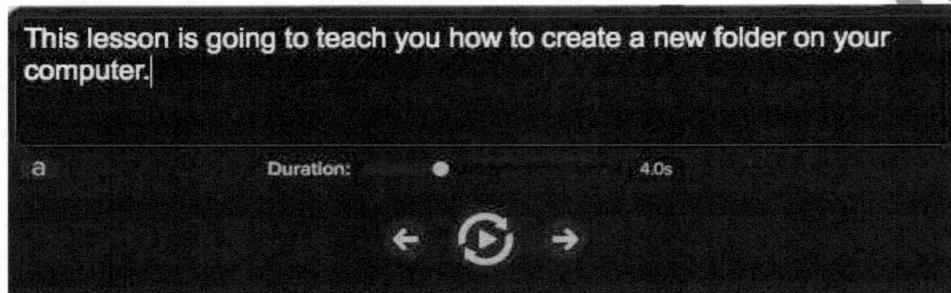

   > This lesson is going to teach you how to create a new folder on your computer.
   >
   > a   Duration: ●   4.0s

2. Export the project to Screencast. (Prior to clicking the Export button, choose **Closed captions** from the **Caption style** drop-down menu.)

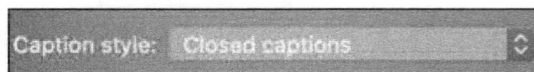

   > Caption style: Closed captions   ↕

3. After the Export process is complete, Visit the page on Screencast.

4. After starting the lesson, click the **CC** button on the playbar to view the captions you added.

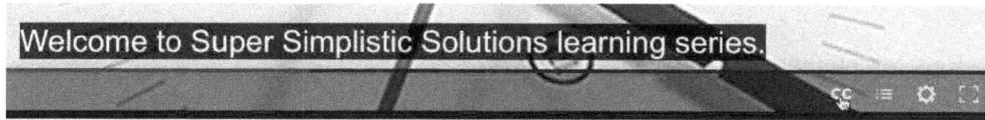

Welcome to Super Simplistic Solutions learning series.

5. Close the browser window.

   Now you'll get a chance to copy and paste text from an existing voiceover script.

6. Hide Camtasia (to get it out of your way for a moment) and, from the Camtasia 2025 Book Assets **> Other_Assets** folder, open **CreatingFoldersVoiceoverScript** with Microsoft Word.

   Audio File 1:
   Welcome to Super Simplistic Solutions learning series.
   This is lesson one: Creating New Folders.

   Audio File 2:
   This lesson is going to teach you how to create a new folder on your computer, how to rename it, and how to both delete and restore recycled items.

   Audio File 3:
   When creating folders keep in mind that you can create as many folders as you need.

   ---

7. In the **Audio File 2** text, select **"how to rename it, and how to both delete and restore recycled items"** and copy the text to the Clipboard.

8. Return to Camtasia and the CaptionMe project.

9. Still working in the second caption, click the right side of the waveform and paste the text you copied into the caption text area.

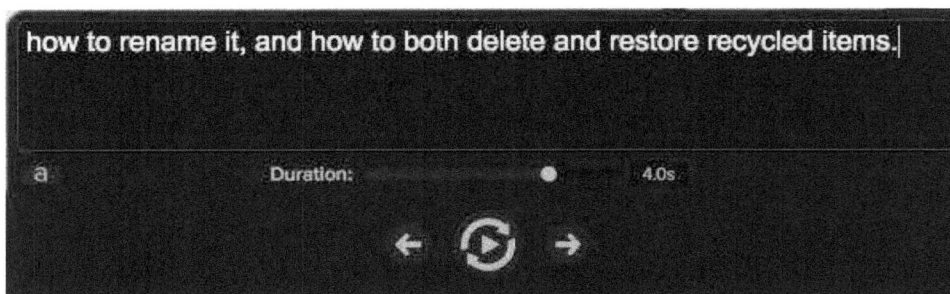

   how to rename it, and how to both delete and restore recycled items.

   a   Duration: ●   4.0s

   ← ⊙ →

10. Save the project.

NOTES

NOTES

Guided Activity 61: Import Captions on the Mac

1. Ensure that the **CaptionMe** project is open.

2. Remove captions.

   ☐ on the **Timeline**, **Captions panel,** click the **Show caption options** icon ⚙ and choose **Remove Captions**

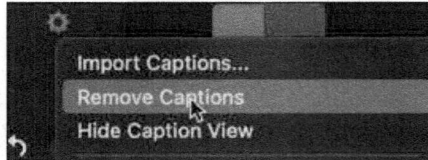

   ☐ click the **OK** button to confirm the action

3. Hide the Captions view.

   ☐ on the **Timeline**, Captions panel, click the **Show caption options** icon ⚙ and choose **Hide Caption View**

4. Import a caption.

   ☐ choose **File > Import > Captions**

   ☐ from **Camtasia 2025 Book Assets > Audio Files > SRT Files**, open **audio_file01.srt**

   The caption is added to Track 4. Because the caption file contains the voiceover script text *and* the timing, the playtime of the caption is an exact match for the audio_file01 media in the voiceover track. The caption just needs to be moved on the Timeline to ensure it appears when the audio begins to play.

5. Reposition a caption on the Timeline.

   ☐ on the **Timeline**, drag the caption in Track 4 **right** until its left edge aligns with the **audio_file01** media in the Voiceover track

6. Import another caption.

   ☐ choose **File > Import > Captions**

   ☐ from **Camtasia 2025 Book Assets > Audio Files > SRT Files**, open **audio_file02.srt**

   The caption is added to Track 5.

7. Reposition the caption on the Timeline.

   ☐ on the **Timeline**, drag the caption in Track 5 **right** until its left edge aligns with the **audio_file02** media in the Voiceover track

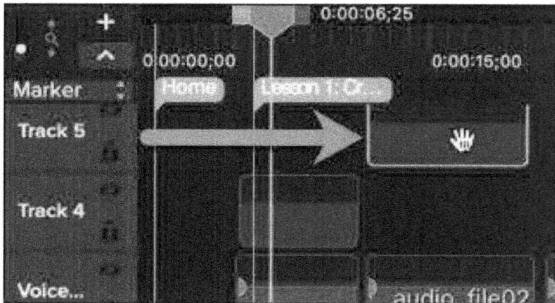

8. Export the project as a Web Page.

9. Once the project has been exported, reveal the exported content in the Finder and open the index.html page.

   You will see that the captions have been automatically added to the output.

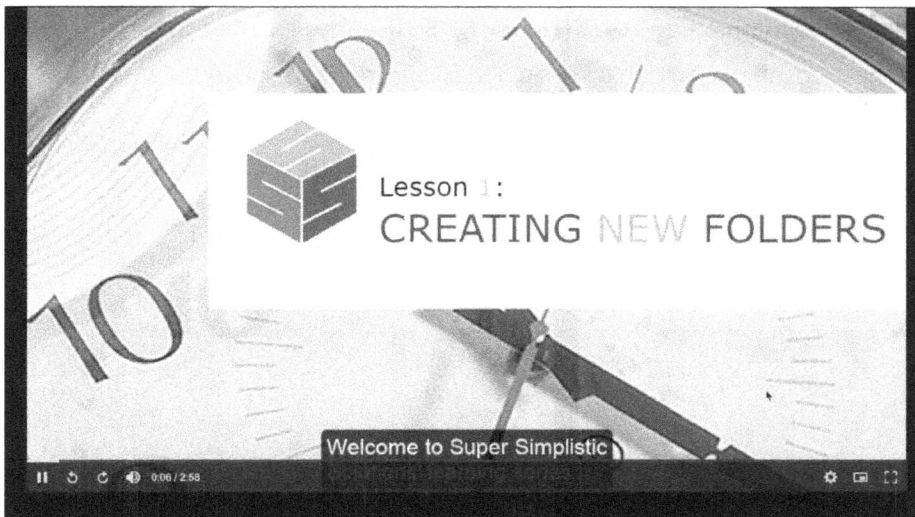

10. Save the project.

NOTES

Guided Activity 62: Create Dynamic Captions on the Mac

1. Ensure that the **CaptionMe** project is open.

2. Remove Track 4.

   ☐ on the Timeline, right-click **Track 4** and choose **Remove**

Track Contains Media

Do you want to delete this track and all media on this track?

OK   Cancel

   ☐ click the **OK** to acknowledge the deletion

The fifth track has been renumbered as Track 4. You do not need this track either.

3. Remove **Track 4** and its media.

4. Open the Dynamic Captions tool.

   ☐ choose **View > Tools > Captions > Dynamic Captions**

The Dynamic Caption Styles open.

5. Add Dynamic Captions.

   ☐ from the **Dynamic Caption Styles** area, select any style that you like
   ☐ **drag** the dynamic caption style onto the Timeline (just above the Voiceover Audio track)

A track is added and captions are created for all of the audio files in the Voiceover Audio track. (Note that this process can take some time.)

   ☐ on the **Timeline**, drag the Dynamic Caption media left to align with the first audio file in the Voiceover Audio track (if necessary)

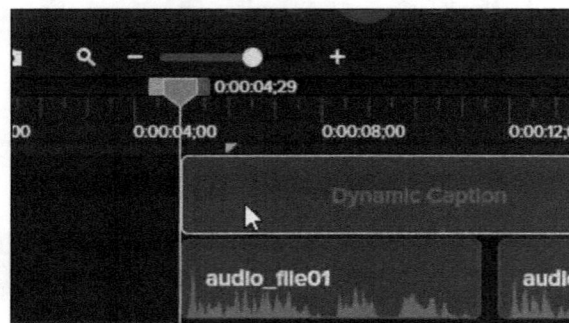

6. On the Canvas, preview the video to see the dynamic captions.

   Note: You can change the appearance of the captions on the Properties panel. You can edit the captions onscreen by clicking the audio media. In the image below, the word "folder" was incorrectly added as "folds." It's simple enough to edit the text as needed.

7. Save the project.

NOTES

NOTES

Templates

Every time you create a new Camtasia project, you're literally starting with a blank canvas. As you've learned during this book, it's easy to fill the Canvas with Library assets, images, annotations, videos, media, and add transitions to media. However, if there are assets and effects that you frequently use in your projects, it's not necessary to start from scratch every time. Instead, you should create a template that contains commonly-used elements. When you create a Camtasia project that uses the template, all of the template's Timeline elements, behaviors, etc., will be retained, saving you time as opposed to starting from scratch.

Guided Activity 63: Create and Use a Template

1. Using Camtasia, create a new project.

2. Add a Library asset to the Timeline.

   ☐ click the **Media** tool at the left and then click **Library**

   ☐ from the **Camtasia 2023** Library assets, open the **Titles** folder

   ☐ right-click **Big Type 1** and choose **Add to Timeline at Playhead**

3. Add a placeholder.

   ☐ position the Playhead at the 20-second mark on the Timeline

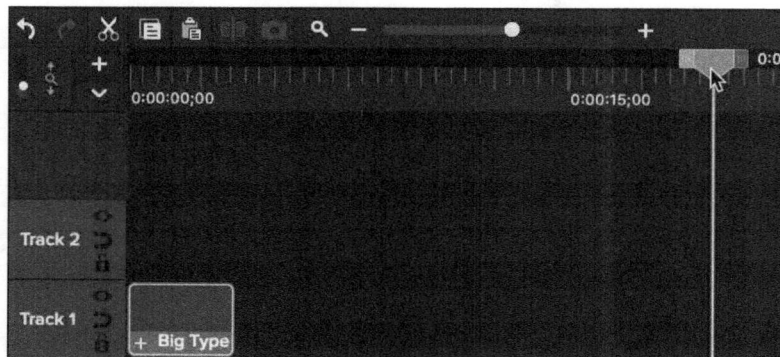

   ☐ choose **Edit > Add Placeholder to Timeline**

A placeholder is an object that can be replaced with any piece of media from the Media Bin, Library, or Annotations. In this instance, the intent is for anyone using your template to replace the placeholder with a screen recording. You'll add instructions next so that anyone using your template knows what to do with the placeholder.

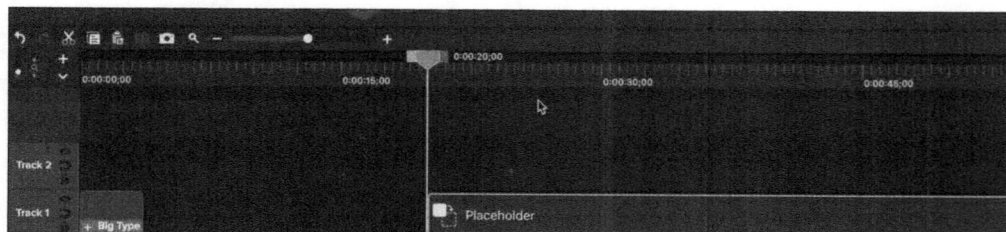

4. Edit Placeholder Properties.

☐ with the Placeholder selected, click in the **Title** area of the Placeholder Properties

☐ type **Screen Recording**

☐ click in the **Notes** field and type **Replace this Placeholder with a screen recording by dragging a video from the Media Bin here.**

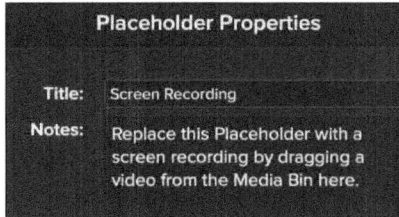

Notice that there's currently a gap between the two Timeline objects, shown highlighted in the image below.

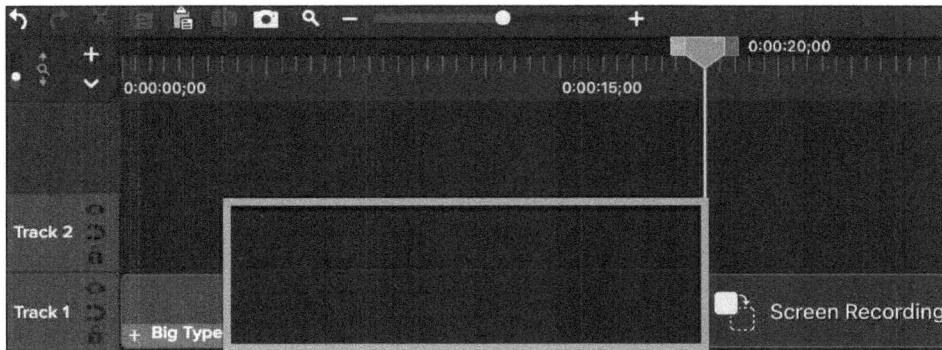

5. Enable Magnetic Tracks.

☐ at the left of **Track 1** on the **Timeline**, click **Enable magnetic track**

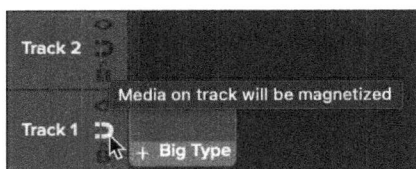

The gap between the Timeline objects is removed.

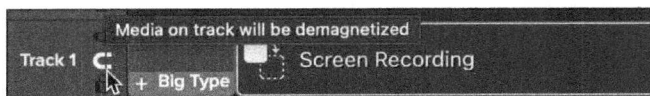

6. Save a project as a template.

☐ choose **File > Save project as template**

The New Template dialog box opens.

NOTES

❑ name the New Template **Recording Template**

❑ click the **OK** button

PC users, You'll be alerted about how to use the template to create a new project. You can acknowledge the alert dialog box by clicking the **OK** button. **Mac users**, close the Untitled project without saving.

7. Create a project based on the new template.

❑ choose **File > New Project from Template**

The Template Manager opens.

❑ select the **Recording Template** you just created
❑ click the **New from Template** button (the button is located in the **bottom right** of the window)

PC users, you'll be prompted to save the project you used to build the template. You can click the **No** button.

A new project is created that has the elements from your template. At this point, you could replace the placeholder text and object with content of your own, just as you have learned to do during lessons throughout this book.

8. Exit/Quit Camtasia. (There is no need to save any open files if prompted.)

That's a Wrap!

Congratulations on completing this book! I hope you enjoyed your learning journey and feel more confident using TechSmith Camtasia. If you need assistance as you continue working with Camtasia, your first stop should be the TechSmith website (http://techsmith.com) and the TechSmith blog (blogs.techsmith.com). TechSmith has a fantastic community where you'll find free tips, tricks, and step-by-step videos on all things Camtasia.

If you are stuck and need a nudge in the right direction, email me at **ksiegel@iconlogic.com**. I offer live, virtual Camtasia training, one-on-one mentoring, custom development services, and both onsite and virtual group training. Learn more at www.iconlogic.com.

Here is a recap of the key concepts you practiced and applied throughout the activities in this book:

Exploring Camtasia

❏ Explore a Completed Camtasia Project, page 12
❏ Explore the Media Bin and Library, page 16
❏ Use the Canvas to Preview a Project, page 19
❏ Use the Canvas Edit and Pan Modes, page 22
❏ Rearrange the Tools, page 23

Recording Videos

❏ Rehearse a Script, page 27
❏ Specify a PC Recording Screen and Size, page 28
❏ Create a Software Video Demo on the PC, page 31
❏ Set Screen Recording Options on the Mac, page 34
❏ Specify a Mac Recording Screen and Size, page 37
❏ Create a Software Video Demo on the Mac, page 40

Adding Media

❏ Create a Project and Edit Project Settings, page 44
❏ Import a Video into the Media Bin, page 45
❏ Add Media to the Timeline and the Canvas, page 47
❏ Import Images to the Media Bin, page 50
❏ Add a Track, page 53
❏ Edit Media Properties, page 56
❏ Add Cursor Effects, page 57
❏ Smooth the Cursor Path, page 60
❏ Edit the Cursor Path, page 64
❏ Control the Cursor Image, Size, and Elevation, page 68

Groups, Annotations, and Animation

❏ Create a Group, page 70
❏ Add a Callout, page 72
❏ Apply and Create Themes, page 75
❏ Apply Image Color to Callout Text, page 79
❏ Add a Behavior to a Callout, page 82
❏ Add a Transition to a Group, page 85
❏ Modify Transition Timing, page 86
❏ Create an Animation, page 87
❏ Use Corner Pin Mode, page 90

Audio

❏ Add Music From the Library, page 94
❏ Import Background Music, page 96

NOTES

NOTES

☐ Fade Audio, page 97
☐ Record Voice Narration, page 100
☐ Split Audio Media, page 103
☐ Rename Tracks, page 105
☐ Silence Audio, Ripple Delete, and Use AI Noise Removal, page 106

Exporting

☐ Export a Project as a Video, page 112
☐ Export a Project as a Website, page 115
☐ Export and Upload to YouTube, page 117
☐ Record Screen Actions with Rev, page 120

Extending, Zooming, and Hotspots

☐ Extend a Video Frame, page 124
☐ Add a Zoom-n-Pan Animation on the PC, page 126
☐ Add a Zoom Animation on the Mac, page 128
☐ Add a Timeline Marker, page 130
☐ Add an Interactive Hotspot, page 133

Quizzes and Reporting Results

☐ Add a Quiz to a Project, page 136
☐ Add a Multiple Choice Question, page 138
☐ Add a Fill In the Blank Question, page 139
☐ Create a Content Package on the PC, page 142
☐ Create a Content Package on the Mac, page 145

PowerPoint, Captions, and Templates

☐ Record PowerPoint on the PC, page 148
☐ Import a PowerPoint Presentation, page 151
☐ Manually Create PC Closed Captions, page 152
☐ Control PC Caption Timing, page 155
☐ Use Speech-to-Text to Create Captions, page 158
☐ Import Captions on the PC, page 160
☐ Create Dynamic Captions on the PC, page 161
☐ Create Mac Closed Captions, page 162
☐ Control Mac Caption Timing, page 166
☐ Import Captions on the Mac, page 168
☐ Create Dynamic Captions on the Mac, page 170
☐ Create and Use a Template, page 172

Index

NOTES

NOTES

NOTES

NOTES

www.ingramcontent.com/pod-product-compliance
Lightning Source LLC
Chambersburg PA
CBHW080545220326
41599CB00032B/6366